EMPIRE
THE UNAUTHORIZED UNTOLD STORY

EMPIRE
THE UNAUTHORIZED UNTOLD STORY

ROBERT HAM

Regan Arts.

NEW YORK

Regan Arts.

65 Bleecker Street
New York, NY 10012

Copyright © 2015 by Regan Arts

First Regan Arts paperback edition, September 2015

Library of Congress Control Number: 2015945681

ISBN 978-1-942872-74-0

Interior design by Nancy Singer
Cover design by Richard Ljoenes
Front cover photograph © Miller Mobley/Redux
Back cover photograph © Ethan Hill/Redux

Printed in the United States of America

10 9 8 7 6 5 4 3 2 1

CONTENTS

Taraji P. Henson and *Empire* co-creator Lee Daniels

THE EPISODES

Empire co-creator Lee Daniels flanked
by Terrence Howard and Taraji P. Henson

BIRTH OF AN EMPIRE

For the past decade or so, network television has been in a rut filled with procedural crime dramas, stale three-camera sitcoms, and warmed-over reality shows that are great if you are white and older than fifty (especially if you are a man). Everybody else has been turning to cable networks like AMC and HBO and their prestige dramas, or binge-watching each new offering from streaming services like Netflix, Hulu, or Amazon Prime. The big five TV networks were missing out on a huge, young, diverse audience, and they needed to find a way to tap into it.

Of course, it's not as if Lee Daniels and Danny Strong were deliberately thinking along those lines when they cooked up *Empire*. All they wanted to do was bring back the seamy thrills of classic 1980s prime-time soaps like *Dynasty* and *Falcon Crest*, but set their story in the modern music world.

As an actor, Danny Strong broke into the industry with a recurring role in the series *Saved by the Bell: The New Class*, and continued to snap up bit parts in films and TV shows for the next decade. His most notable roles came thanks to big story arcs in *Buffy the Vampire Slayer* (as one of a trio of gents trying to stir up magical trouble in Sunnydale) and *Gilmore Girls* (playing Doyle, the *Yale Daily News* editor and on-again, off-again love interest of the tightly wound Paris). Later, he had a memorable role as one of the creatives working for Sterling Cooper Draper Pryce on *Mad Men*. All that time, though, he was putting together an impressive résumé of work behind the camera as a screenwriter and producer, including an Emmy for his work on *Game Change*, the HBO film about John McCain and Sarah Palin's failed presidential campaign, and a Writers Guild Award for *Recount*, another cable movie about the controversial and chaotic presidential election of 2000.

The initial idea for *Empire* came to him, he recalled in an interview for the podcast *The Business*, as he was driving around Los Angeles one day. "I heard a news story about Puffy, and I just thought, 'Hip-hop is so cool. That's what I should do next, something in hip-hop.'" From there, his imagination took a historical turn, to the royal intrigues of plays like Shakespeare's *King Lear* and James Goldman's *The Lion in Winter*. Could he take the dramatic family conflicts of those stories, which pit husbands against wives and sons and daughters against their parents, and transplant them to the contemporary world of hip-hop?

To help him turn this stray idea into a reality, Strong called his friend Lee Daniels, with whom he'd recently worked as the screenwriter for *The Butler*, the hit historical drama starring Forest Whitaker and Oprah Winfrey. Daniels was enjoying a career high after living through the kind of pull-yourself-up-by-the-bootstraps story that inspires hundreds of people every year to move to Los Angeles in hopes of making a splash in the entertainment industry. Instead of going to film school, the former Philadelphia native had worked his way up the ranks as a manager and a casting director; one of his first big breaks was working with Prince to find actors for music videos and the film *Under the Cherry Moon*. Eventually, he moved up to producing feature films, including the award-winning dramas *Monster's Ball* and *The Woodsman*. Although his directorial debut, *Shadowboxer*, didn't make a big splash, his next project—an adaptation of Sapphire's novel *Push* retitled *Precious*—won awards at Sundance and Cannes and earned him a Best Director nomination at the Academy Awards. (The film's young lead, Gabourey Sidibe, was also nominated for Best Actress, and her costar Mo'Nique took home the award for Best Supporting Actress.)

After a small critical and commercial setback with the 2012 release of his adaptation of the novel *The Paperboy*, Daniels returned in a big way with *The Butler*. Though it didn't earn the accolades that *Precious* did, the film earned more than $150 million and nabbed several nominations for Screen Actors Guild and Critics' Choice Awards. And he felt an immediate kinship with Danny Strong from the moment they began working together. "I think we are kindred spirits artistically," Strong told *Out* magazine. "We're kind of polar opposites in personalities but I think creatively we are kindred spirits. We both like our stories to be entertaining and bombastic but also important and with depth. Neither of us are afraid to go there."

Empire co-creator Danny Strong

When Strong approached Daniels with the kernel of an idea for *Empire*, the screenwriter was initially thinking that it would be another film project for them to work on. Still smarting from the hurdles he'd had to go through to get *The Butler* off the ground, and wanting to earn a little extra cash this time around, the director suggested they turn this project into a TV series that recreated the dramatic beats of prime-time soaps like *Dynasty* and *Knots Landing*.

When they had finished writing the pilot episode, though, Daniels and Strong were unsure whether America was really ready for a show like this. "I felt very similarly to when I walked away from *Precious*," Daniels told the *Los Angeles Times*. "I felt naked; I felt vulnerable. I felt I didn't know if I want white

America seeing this; I didn't know if I want black America exposed like this. It was an uncomfortable feeling."

Even with his concerns, Daniels and Strong still had a lot of heat in the industry thanks to the success of *The Butler*. That was, in part, what helped Brian Grazer agree to lend the juice of his company Imagine Entertainment to the project. Another key factor in Grazer's decision, as he later told attendees of the Produced By Conference in Los Angeles, was Strong's description of *Empire* in the pitch meeting: "Danny gave me the headline of '*King Lear* in the world of hip-hop,'" Grazer recalled, "and I knew very little about *King Lear*, but I did know all about hip-hop."

As word spread that Daniels and Strong were headed to television and had Imagine backing them, a bidding war broke out over *Empire*. Fox won, even trumping offers from some cable networks, because, as Daniels said to the *Hollywood Reporter*, "Most of my relatives can't afford cable, but they can afford Fox. [And] Fox would let me be me as much as they could let me be me."

Letting Daniels be Daniels might just be the best decision the network made all year, with dividends nobody had anticipated. From the moment the pilot episode aired on January 7, 2015, *Empire* immediately bucked every ratings trend imaginable. The show was watched by twice as many women as men, in particular drawing in African American women—who, according to *Vulture*, helped the series score higher ratings than some of that month's NFL playoff games. The show also scored twice as many viewers as any other scripted drama on Fox in Hispanic households. Most important, the coveted eighteen-to-forty-nine demographic kept returning week after week, either watching the show as it aired, catching it on their DVRs, or checking out episodes as they made their way online.

Television shows just aren't supposed to take off the way *Empire* has. Even a modern classic like *Breaking Bad* started out with just more than one million viewers when its first episode aired on AMC. Five years later, when Walter White met his fate in the series finale, more than ten million people were tuned in. When Fox dropped *Empire* into its prime-time schedule, the network seemed to be planning for a similar slow build, tucking it into the Wednesday night lineup behind *American Idol*. They must have figured the audience for the long-running singing competition might stick around for a modern-day soap opera rooted in the world of hip-hop.

For the first episode, that strategy certainly worked. The season premiere of *American Idol*'s fourteenth season drew in more than eleven million viewers, enabling Fox to dominate the hour; and nearly ten million of them stayed with the network and got to meet cold-hearted music legend Lucious Lyon, his three sons, and Cookie, his sassy and sexy ex-wife. *Empire* was the highest-watched show that hour, beating out episodes of *Modern Family* and *Law & Order: SVU*, as well as the People's Choice Awards.

What happened next was, as one Fox executive admitted to the *Los Angeles Times*, "[an] amazing, phenomenal trajectory that defies all laws of television." The ratings for *Empire* increased steadily, week after week—the first time any network series had been able to accomplish such a feat in more than two decades—to the point where seventeen and a half million people watched the two-part season finale in mid-March. "We're all very excited about it," Brian Grazer confided in that same *Los Angeles Times* story, "but we had no idea it would do as well as it's doing."

In retrospect, though, it's not quite so difficult to understand why *Empire* took off the way it did. As Andy Greenwald wrote in an article on the show for Grantland.com, "In order to succeed in America, you have to have shows that, you know, endeavor to actually look like America." Unlike most network dramas, where they sprinkle in a few nonwhite actors and call themselves "diverse," almost all the main characters on *Empire* are people of color. It's also a show that takes its female characters very seriously, not just reducing them to background figures meant to titillate male fans (though, to be fair, there's still some of that happening, too). Cookie, Anika, and Rhonda are all strong, fierce women with sharp business acumen, sharper tongues, and lots of form-fitting outfits. For all the sometimes-troubling decisions they made as the first season's storyline unfolded, these characters were aspirational figures for many of *Empire*'s female viewers. "Cookie walks in truth and I think that's why people are gravitating towards her," actress Taraji P. Henson told the *London Evening Standard*, "because she does and says the things that people are afraid to do and say."

This also being the age of the meme, *Empire*'s steep rise in ratings also owes a debt to the world of social media. As TV critic Gilbert Cruz wrote for the *New York Times*, the show "played to the digital seats," noting Cookie's sharp, quotable dialogue (like her use of the popular online dismissal "Bye, Felicia!" in one scene). "It's a sign of the Internet savvy of the show's creators," he added, "aware of how social media–ready moments can help propel a show to greater heights."

Such great heights, in fact, that the two-hour series finale generated more than two million tweets from fans and also drew a lot of attention to the cast members' personal Twitter accounts. As they gathered at Fox's offices to live-tweet the second-to-last episode together, each one saw a gigantic spike in followers. Jussie Smollett picked up 150,000 new followers that evening, and Taraji P. Henson expanded her already huge follower list by 39,000. Others saw exponential Twitter growth over the course of the season, with Grace Gealey (Anika Calhoun on the show) going from just less than 400 followers to more than 65,000, and Trai Byers (Andre Lyon) seeing more than 75,000 followers jump on board through the early part of 2015.

Another significant element in the show's success is the music that permeates every episode. As much as pundits like Bill O'Reilly don't want to hear it, hip-hop is still the driving force in our culture, influencing fashion, art, and films—now here was a TV show featuring real-deal rap and R&B tunes, written and produced by well-known names like Timbaland, Raphael Saadiq, Christopher

"Tricky" Stewart, and Jim Beanz. These songs sounded like they should be chart toppers in the world of *Empire*, and when they were released online after each episode aired, they became hits in the real world, too. At the end of the season, the *Empire* soundtrack immediately debuted at #1 on the *Billboard* album charts.

Now, everyone in television will scramble to replicate *Empire*'s success, but what they're likely to overlook as they try is one of the most fundamental aspects of the show's appeal: it is just flat out *fun* to watch. The drama in every episode is heightened to an almost absurd level, with multiple cliffhangers, surprise reveals, and moments of raw anger or sensuality crafted to keep us caught up in the show's world from start to finish. And you just can't plan for the way a character like Cookie—a slinky, catty, and street-smart woman with a penchant for bursting into any room she's not supposed to be in while leveling anyone in her way with a contemptuous look or a quick verbal slap—breaks out of the pack and becomes a fan favorite.

That also puts a lot of pressure on *Empire* to be even bigger with its second season. The folks behind the show are certainly doing their part to make that a reality. The cast worked overtime to promote *Empire* over the summer, including appearances by Smollett, Yazz the Greatest, and Serayah at the BET Awards. Meanwhile, the *Empire* Twitter feed, Snapchat account, and Tumblr page have remained active, whetting fans' appetites with GIFs, memes, and a countdown toward the season premiere.

They're wise to keep pushing rather than just expecting old fans to return and stick with the show this fall, while hoping new viewers will jump aboard the train. That said, *Empire did* defy all forecasts for its first season and wound up shifting our cultural conversation, week after groundbreaking week. What's to stop them from doing it all over again?

The Lyon brothers: Trai Byers (Andre), Jussie Smollett (Jamal), and Bryshere Y. Gray (Hakeem)

WHO'S
WHO

LUCIOUS LYON

The founder and CEO of Empire Enterprises has a backstory that should sound familiar to anyone who has followed the career trajectory of artists like Jay Z, The Notorious B.I.G., or Rick Ross. Born in Philadelphia, Lyon (born Dwight Walker) started selling drugs at the very tender age of nine. Initially, the move was simply to help him survive on the streets of his hometown after being orphaned, but as his interest in making music grew, it became a means to an end. By all accounts, Lyon is deeply talented. He has a keen ear for arrangement and melodies, remarkable skills on both the piano and the guitar, and one hell of a singing voice. With the money he earned dealing crack and cocaine, he was able to fund his career as a musician and a producer.

Using the marketing expertise he picked up in the drug trade, Lyon started to build some buzz selling his self-produced and self-financed CDs at barbershops and strip clubs around Philly. It was through this hustling that he met Loretha Holloway, better known as Cookie. The two quickly became partners in life and in business. As she raised their three sons—Andre, Jamal, and Hakeem—Cookie also supported Lucious's efforts as both a dealer and a musician. In fact, if it weren't for Cookie, Lucious wouldn't have a career to speak of. Not only did she help generate the seed money for what would become Empire Enterprises, but after her arrest for dealing, she refused to implicate her husband lest it hurt his chances at success.

Cookie is just one of many individuals who helped Lucious in the formation of his entertainment dynasty. After Cookie's arrest, Lucious turned to his wife's cousin Bunkie and his lifelong best friend, Vernon, for help raising his kids, while Billy Beretti and Creedmoor Records gave his music career an invaluable boost. With Creedmoor's backing, Lucious went from being a hometown hero to an internationally known superstar, thanks to albums like *2-1-5 or Die* and *That's What the DJ Spins*.

One of Lucious's most troubling qualities is his coldheartedness, a cutthroat mentality that slashes through anyone who might impede his path to the top. In his drug-slinging days, he conspired with his cousin to have a pair of rival dealers murdered. Later on, he clashed publicly with Beretti over the sound of his music and the money he was earning from it, leading to an acrimonious split with Creedmoor. Most heartbreaking, Lucious decided to cut all ties with Cookie, sending her divorce papers while she languished in prison.

As tough as those tactics were, they helped clear the way for him to build a multimedia kingdom. Alongside releasing his own work, Lucious started mentoring and supporting other artists, including Wallywowwow, soul singer Elle Dallas, Kidd Fo-Fo, and the Hunts Point Blank Trio, along with his two musically talented sons, Jamal and Hakeem.

By the time we catch up with Lucious in the first episode of *Empire*, his record company has grown into a multimillion-dollar global brand that extends to a clothing line and top-shelf liquors, with recent expansion into developing video games and managing the careers of athletes. That's why, at the start of the show, Lyon and his board of directors are ready to take Empire Enterprises public, anticipating a multibillion-dollar windfall.

Prior to the announcement, though, things start to get incredibly complicated in Lucious's life. First he is diagnosed with amyotrophic lateral sclerosis (ALS, also known as Lou Gehrig's disease), a neurological disorder with no known cure that weakens the muscles and nervous system. Then his ex-wife is released from prison after seventeen years and wants to be part of the action at Empire. If that weren't enough, Cookie's cousin Bunkie starts making veiled threats, looking to extort money from Lucious to pay off his gambling debts. With all that going on, how can he decide which of his three sons will take over the company after his death? So much drama, but as you know, that's what *Empire* is all about.

Terrence Howard

When Lee Daniels was first thinking about who would take on the role of Lucious Lyon, the writer/director imagined hiring veteran actor Wesley Snipes—but, he says, Taraji P. Henson told him she wouldn't take the part of Cookie unless she could play opposite Terrence Howard.

Lucky for us, Daniels trusted his actress's instincts. Howard turned out to be perfectly cast as the complex and talented Lucious Lyon, capable of bringing alive the character's intense drama, sly humor, and smoldering sensuality—not to mention his great singing voice.

Born in Chicago in March 1969, Howard was inspired to try his hand at drama thanks to his great-grandmother, Minnie Gentry, who spent most of her career acting on Broadway and in small roles on *The Cosby Show* and in films such as *The Brother from Another Planet* and *Bad Lieutenant*. Along the way, Howard also learned to play guitar, cultivating dreams of being a musician.

It wasn't until the early '90s that Howard finally landed some acting work, starting with a role as one of the Jackson 5 in a TV miniseries. For a decade following that, he kept up a steady stream of performances, including supporting roles in Ice Cube's directorial debut, *The Players Club*, in 1999's *Best Laid Plans*, and in an acclaimed performance in the 1999 romantic comedy *The Best Man*, which netted him his first NAACP Image Award.

Howard broke out in a big way in 2005, playing the pimp-turned-rapper Djay in the film *Hustle & Flow*. His star-making performance earned him a raft of awards and a nomination for Best Actor at that year's Academy Awards. Since then, he's taken on parts as high profile as Tony Stark's best friend, James Rhodes, in the first *Iron Man* film and as Nelson Mandela in the 2011 film *Winnie Mandela* and as small as his supporting work in the film adaptation of Jack Kerouac's *On the Road* and the acclaimed indie *St. Vincent*.

The biggest challenges in Howard's life, however, have happened offscreen. He was replaced by Don Cheadle in the *Iron Man* sequels after refusing to take a substantial pay cut to reprise his role from the first film. Howard also has a troubling reputation for violence. In 2000, he was accused of assaulting a flight attendant; and five years later, he attacked a couple at a Philadelphia restaurant when they were seated ahead of him. Even worse, Howard admits to having punched his first wife, Lori McCommas, in the face, and has been accused of doing the same to his second wife, Michelle Ghent.

The Real-Life
LUCIOUS LYON?

There's been plenty of speculation about the inspiration for Lucious, with *Empire* cocreator Lee Daniels stirring the pot a bit by telling the *Philadelphia Inquirer* that the character is a mixture of "men I've respected over the years, from Berry Gordy to Gamble and Huff to Jay Z to Puffy to Quincy Jones." While there is one parallel between Lucious and Jay Z (left)—both men built their now-lucrative careers after years of drug dealing—that's pretty much where the comparisons run out. There could also be a bit of P. Diddy in the mix, as rumors have swirled about the Bad Boy Entertainment impresario's son having a homosexual relationship, like Lucious's son Jamal. Again, though, it's a pretty flimsy connection—though there *was* talk about Sean Combs (right) considering a lawsuit against the creators of *Empire* for supposedly stealing his "life story."

"I started selling drugs when I was nine years old in Philadelphia. I did it to feed myself. But it was the music that played in my head that kept me alive when I thought I was gonna get shot. And it was the melodies that I dreamt about that kept me warm while I was sleeping in the streets. You see, **MUSIC SAVED MY LIFE.**"

"REGARDLESS OF HOW WE FIGHT OR WE FEEL ABOUT EACH OTHER OR TRY TO HURT EACH OTHER, THE MUSIC, MAN. MUSIC, THAT'S FOREVER. THEY'LL DANCE TO IT FOREVER. THEY'LL SING TO IT FOREVER. THEY'LL BE INSPIRED BY IT FOREVER. PUT THE BAD BLOOD BEHIND US. TELL YOUR TRUTH IN THE MUSIC."

"When a man in my position says **'PLEASE,'** it means something. When a man like me says 'hear me out,' you hear me out, 'cause your life could depend on it."

"Witness as Empire becomes synonymous with American culture."

COOKIE LYON

Not much is known about Loretha "Cookie" Holloway's life before she became the wife of notorious Philadelphia drug dealer and hip-hop artist Lucious Lyon. But if her hard-nosed personality and quick wit are anything to go by, she surely wasn't someone you'd want to mess with.

When she did meet up with her future husband, she quickly became an ally, helping him deal cocaine and crack, and using the profits —$400,000, as she often reminds Lucious and their sons—to help get his recording career and label off the ground. Cookie also proved herself indispensible in the studio, using her keen ear for a potential hit to assist her husband's songwriting efforts. If that weren't enough, she also gave birth to three boys and helped raise them while keeping both business ventures alive.

She is perhaps a little too helpful, though. When she was nabbed by the police for possession with intent to distribute (likely tipped off by a rival dealer), Cookie refused to roll over on her husband or anyone else in the business, landing herself in the penitentiary for seventeen years. Survivor that she is, Cookie handled herself very well, taking out any fellow inmates who dared step to her and finding a few romantic partners on the inside.

True to her married surname, Cookie bursts out with feline ferocity once she is released. She storms into the world of Empire Enterprises sporting an array of skintight animal-print outfits, demanding to be compensated for her initial investment with half the company while also slicing and dicing her way past her ex-husband's new lady friend, Anika, with cutting remarks and a bit of physical intimidation. Cookie gets right to work, with plans to turn out a bevy of chart-topping stars, including her conflicted, closeted son, Jamal, and the former cornerstone act in Empire's arsenal, Elle Dallas. If she manages to mend fences with her three sons and possibly lure Lucious back into her arms, all the better.

If she has any other concern outside of her interest in taking back what's hers and proving her worth at Empire, it's the federal agent who keeps popping up at the most inopportune times to insist Cookie inform on a former rival in the drug trade. Informing may have helped secure her an early release, but she could be potentially risking her life by snitching on someone else in the game.

Taraji P. Henson

Born in Washington, DC, in 1970 and given a first name that means "hope" in Swahili, Taraji P. Henson didn't have her mind on acting when she left home for college, instead studying (and failing) math and electrical engineering. That stumble ended up being a blessing in disguise, as it forced her to transfer her education to Howard University, where she studied acting and paid her way through college by working as a secretary at the Pentagon and as a singing waitress on a dinner cruise ship.

After graduating, Henson left for Los Angeles. She subsisted on TV and film work before landing her first breakout role in the 2001 coming-of-age film *Baby Boy*, in which she plays the girlfriend and baby mama of Tyrese Gibson's lead character. More acclaim came her way in 2005 for her portrayal of the pregnant ex-prostitute Shug, alongside her future *Empire* costar Terrence Howard, in *Hustle & Flow*. The role took Henson to the Academy Awards to perform "It's Hard out Here for a Pimp" with Best Original Song nominees Three 6 Mafia. Three years later, she was back as a nominee in her own right, up for Best Supporting Actress for her moving portrayal of Queenie, the maidservant to the title character in *The Curious Case of Benjamin Button*.

Unlike many of her costars on *Empire*, Henson is no stranger to regular television work, with notable arcs on the Lifetime series *The Division* and ABC's courtroom drama *Boston Legal*. She also starred as Detective Joss Carter in the CBS crime series *Person of Interest*, though that gig was unceremoniously cut short when her character was killed at the midpoint of the show's third season. Their loss was *Empire*'s gain, as Lee Daniels was able to snap up Henson just a few months later to play the much juicier role of Cookie Lyon.

The Real-Life
COOKIE LYON?

According to Lee Daniels, the character of Cookie Lyon is based more on figures from his own life than anyone in the music industry. He named the character after his cousin, and told the *Philadelphia Inquirer* that Cookie's personality is an amalgam of that cousin as well as being based "on a close friend, and on a lot of the women I knew growing up." If we're speculating, though, the person in the music industry who most nearly fits Cookie's combination of musical smarts and tough-as-nails attitude might be Lil' Kim (left). The rapper has had her own relationship with a famous recording artist (The Notorious B.I.G.) and legal troubles, including a one-year stint in prison for lying to a grand jury while trying to protect friends involved in a shooting outside a New York City radio station in 2001. The *New York Post* also put forth their own candidate, suggesting former Sugar Hill Records founder Sylvia Robinson (right), who helped kick off the careers of Grandmaster Flash and the Treacherous Three, as a potential source of inspiration.

"You can fool this country you legit, but I know you ain't nothing but a PUNK-ASS GANGSTA."

"You want Cookie's nookie, ditch the bitch."

"Tell me why I shouldn't throw this drink in your BITCH-ASS FACE."

"YEAH, DIFFICULT. I KNOW THAT WORD. YOU SEE, Y'ALL LIKE TO TOSS US TO THE SIDE WHEN YOU CAN'T CONTROL US ANYMORE, BECAUSE YOU'RE LAZY AND YOU DON'T WANT TO DO YOUR JOB."

JAMAL LYON

In all children's lives, there are moments that cement their view of the world and set the stage for many of their future relationships. For Jamal Lyon, it was the night he decided to try on some of his mother's clothes and a pair of her high heels. When the young man walked downstairs to present himself to his parents, Lucious freaked out, carrying his son outside and shoving him in a trash can. Is it any wonder that as he grew older and started to make a name for himself as a singer and songwriter, Jamal decided to keep his homosexuality hidden?

It didn't help that Jamal faced ridicule and abuse at school as well, hardening the young man's heart even more and giving a cynical edge to his day-to-day interactions with the world. The anchor keeping him grounded through it all, though, has been his family. He and his brothers, Hakeem and Andre, formed a tight-knit circle as they grew up, a bond that keeps getting restrengthened even as things become more frayed within the hierarchy of Empire Enterprises. Jamal was also one of the few members of the family to pay regular visits to prison to see Cookie.

The only person Jamal continues to distrust and, in a lot of ways, fear is his father. That night when Lucious revealed his feelings about his son's budding homosexuality drove a wedge between the two that has yet to be fully removed. Their relationship is further complicated by Lucious's financial support for his son and his efforts to use his clout in the music industry to make Jamal a star.

Again, Jamal's fearfulness at how people will react to his music and image has played a huge part in why he has yet to become widely known in the R&B world. Though his songs are being released and generating a bit of interest, he won't play the game, refusing to do any big promotional appearances or touring to support his work.

At the start of the series, all of these issues are coming to a head. As Jamal wrestles with his devotion to his father and the family, Cookie storms back into his world, promising to help cultivate his artistic vision. That puts him even more at odds with his father, as Lucious is still refusing to acknowledge his son's homosexuality or even the existence of Jamal's partner, Michael.

The news that Lucious is going to choose one of his sons to take over the company throws every relationship in the family into disarray, with Jamal, Andre, and Hakeem all gaming for a shot at the throne while also trying to maintain the close connection they share. At least Jamal and Hakeem have the music to help keep them tied together. Throughout the series, the two are constantly collaborating, mixing up modern R&B and hip-hop in some of the show's most memorable songs.

Jussie Smollett

Born into a family of actors in California in 1983, Jussie Smollett began his career at a young age, landing a part in a TV movie when he was just eight years old. Soon he was booking even higher-profile gigs, with parts in *The Mighty Ducks* and a TV-miniseries adaptation of Alex Haley's novel *Queen: The Story of an American Family* alongside Halle Berry and Danny Glover. Smollett even got to work with his five siblings when they were all cast in the short-lived ABC sitcom *On Our Own*.

Smollett took a short break in the late 1990s and early 2000s to concentrate on his studies but has been back in the acting game with a series of small television appearances and roles in a few lesser-known independent films. Playing Jamal on *Empire* has been the real catalyst in bringing him well-deserved recognition from fans, a lot of critical acclaim, and even a few award nominations. His singing and songwriting skills—he cowrote "You're So Beautiful" and "I Wanna Love You"—have also earned him a recording contract with Columbia. Unlike his character, Smollett has never shied away from his own homosexuality, or as he put it during an appearance on *The Ellen DeGeneres Show*, "There's never been a closet that I've been in."

The Real-Life
JAMAL LYON?

Though Diddy may be convinced that the character is based on one of his sons, Jamal's struggles as a gay man are rooted in experiences from *Empire* cocreator Lee Daniels's life. The scene when Lucious angrily deposits his son in a trash can? That really happened to Daniels as a child.

Looking at the music industry, the closest parallel out there for a conflicted and talented person like Jamal may be Frank Ocean (left). The beloved singer/songwriter stirred up a lot of conversation in 2012 when he published a letter on Tumblr that discussed his deep love for a young man he met in his teens. Ocean has been mostly cagey about his sexuality since then, but his willingness to explore these issues in a public forum certainly helped set a precedent for a character like Jamal in a major TV show.

"My obedience is no longer for sale."

"MOM, I'M TELLING YOU RIGHT NOW, JUST BE
CAREFUL. YOU DO NOT WANT TO LOVE THAT
MAN. BECAUSE HE'S INCAPABLE OF LOVING
ANYBODY BUT HIMSELF."

"All my life, all I ever
wanted was for that man
to LOVE ME."

"Put aside your played-out
homophobia unless it's more
important to you than Empire."

HAKEEM LYON

The youngest of Lucious and Cookie Lyon's three sons, Hakeem has had possibly a tougher time growing up than either of his siblings. If only because when he was a baby, his father had to leave him in the care of others while his career was starting to explode and Hakeem's mother was behind bars. While that has made for a fraught relationship between Hakeem and Cookie, it also only toughened Hakeem's resolve and has made him even more determined to prove himself to his father as a rapper.

Like a lot of other young, headstrong rhymers, Hakeem is easily seduced by the trappings of his father's success and the indulgences that come along with it. He's the flashiest of any of the Lyon boys, with plenty of bling to show for it, and has a healthy appetite for drink, drugs, and women. As talented as he is on the mic, his entitled attitude has also made him increasingly lazy, so he leans hard on his older brother Jamal to help him write new songs.

What has become apparent throughout the first season is how much Hakeem can pull out of himself if he digs deep. Challenged in the studio by his father

and brothers, he can spin off verses that are streetwise, witty, and a little melancholy. Trouble is, Hakeem has a tendency for self-sabotage. He got caught on video dissing his white fans and Barack Obama, and found himself juggling relationships with Empire Enterprises' newest signing, Tiana, and the fashion designer Camilla Marks. For all his street smarts, he is proving to be incredibly dumb about a lot of things, putting him at a distinct disadvantage when it comes to his chances at taking over as CEO of Empire Enterprises.

Bryshere Y. Gray

Bryshere Y. Gray is one of the youngest regular cast members on the show—*Empire* is actually his first acting gig. The Philadelphian is best known for his rap career as Yazz the Greatest (riffing off his middle name, Yazshawn), which began when he was sixteen. After breaking his arm playing high school football, Gray became obsessed with hip-hop and used his newly found free time to start writing his own rhymes and cooking up his own music. He was savvy enough to realize that he could earn some money to help his mother pay the bills by performing on the street for passersby, and from there he quickly started to get bigger and bigger bookings, including a spot at the Roots Picnic, the annual event thrown by the Philly-born house band for *The Tonight Show*.

His acting career is, as Lee Daniels puts it, "a Cinderella story." The casting agents for *Empire* saw hundreds of upstart rappers try out for the part of Hakeem, but they fell for Gray after he was flown to Los Angeles (his first time on an airplane) and auditioned with Taraji P. Henson and Terrence Howard. As Gray told HipHopDX.com, "They loved it and that was literally my first time acting. It was all instinct."

The Real-Life

HAKEEM LYON?

While Vulture.com suggests Hakeem's character is mostly based on Diggy Simmons (right), the wannabe rapper who failed to launch a music career after he appeared on the reality show *Run's House* with his father (Rev Run of Run-DMC fame), that's not giving Hakeem enough credit for his skills. Really, it feels like he could have much more in common with Tyga (left), the California-based rhymer best known for his relationship with another reality show star, Kylie Jenner, and for offstage activities that include producing porn films such as *Rack City XXX*.

"I don't wanna win the game.
I wanna change it."

"I'm not
watering
my music
down for
NO TWEENS."

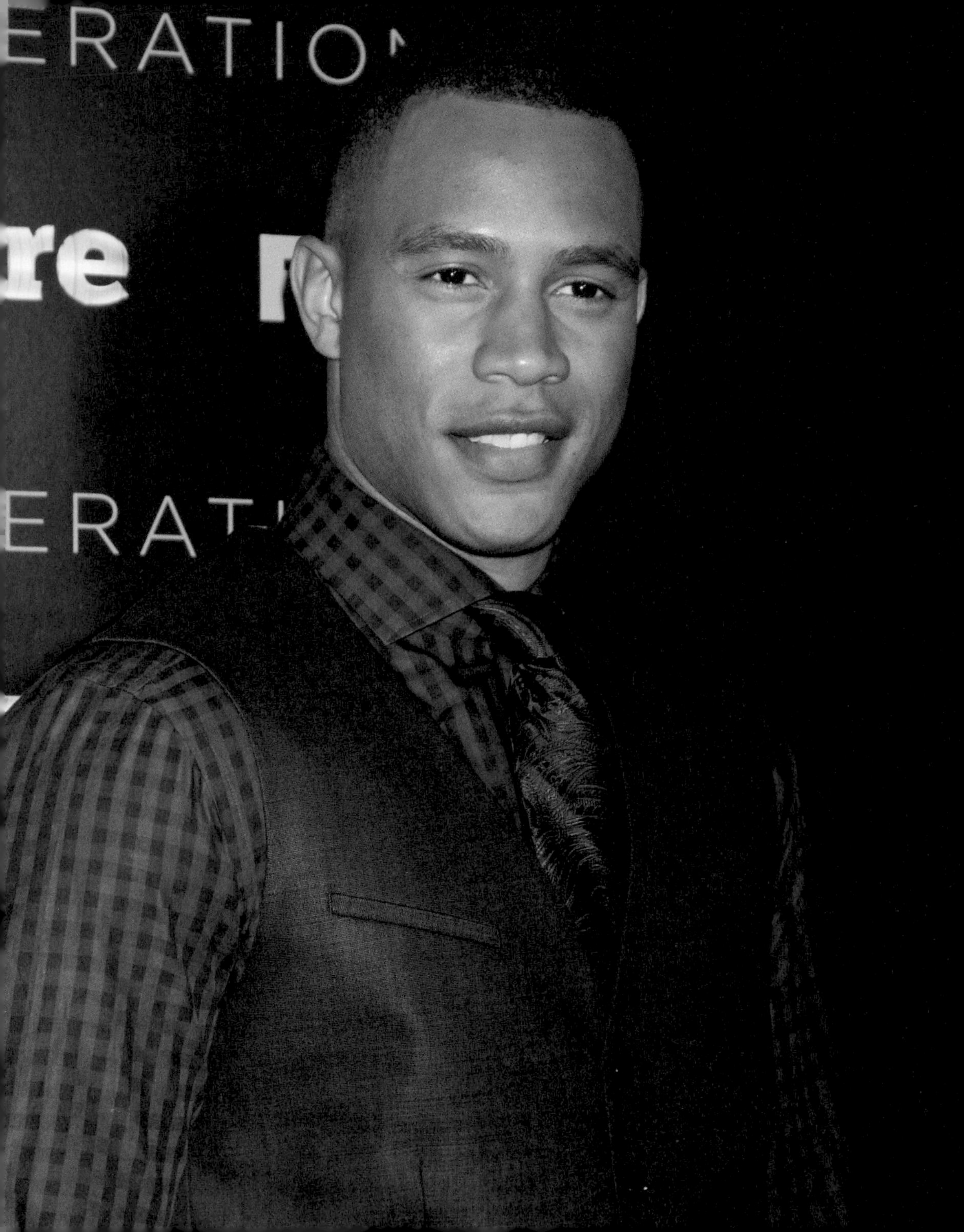
ERATION
re
ERATI

ANDRE LYON

L ike his younger brother Jamal, Andre Lyon had a formative experience at an early age that has defined his role within the family ever since. Tipped off that the police were about to raid his home, Lucious quickly began hiding any contraband, including an illegal handgun. In his hurried state, he put the pistol in a spot where it was sure to be found. Ten-year-old Andre could see that the weapon would be uncovered, so he took it and stashed it in a box of Legos until the police left.

As CFO of Empire Enterprises, Andre continues to do the dirty work necessary to give his father, brothers, and their roster of artists the freedom to make art and a whole lot of money. When the company is set to go public, it's Andre who sacrifices his mental well-being in an effort to keep the leaky ship afloat amid various crises and scandals, including Cookie's return. It's an especially thankless job considering he is the one member of the family with no musical talent (a particularly sore subject for the business-minded executive).

His psychological health is the biggest challenge to his efforts to prove himself worthy of taking over as Empire's CEO. Diagnosed as bipolar, Andre has a tendency to skip his meds, putting himself and his family at risk. In keeping with the Lyon family tradition of keeping secrets from the rest of the clan, he has spent a long time keeping his condition a secret, and only his wife, Rhonda, is aware of how shaky his situation is.

Andre also exhibits some of his father's more conspiratorial personality traits, covering for Lucious when the cops come calling to question him about the death of Bunkie Williams, played by Antoine McKay, claiming that they had spent that evening watching a boxing match together. Throughout *Empire*'s first season, Andre pits his brothers against each other, going so far as to encourage Hakeem's entourage to rob the studio where Jamal is recording new material. Andre is playing a dangerous game, but he wouldn't be a Lyon if he didn't.

Trai
Byers

Trai Byers has landed some fairly remarkable acting gigs in his short career. Born in Kansas City,
Kansas, in 1983, he devoted much of his time to
school, graduating from the University of Kansas
and then going on to study acting at the Yale
School of Drama and the American Musical and
Dramatic Academy in Los Angeles. Not long after,
Byers scored some TV work, with recurring roles
on the long-running soap opera *All My Children*
and the reboot of *90210*, and was subsequently
cast in the civil rights drama *Selma*, in which he
portrayed noted activist James Forman.

The Real-Life
ANDRE LYON?

No one disputes that one of the key sources of inspiration for the character of Andre Lyon is hip-hop entrepreneur Damon "Dame" Dash (left), who worked closely with Jay Z in the founding of Roc-A-Fella Records—and, like Andre, eventually found himself on the outs with his former associate. After helping Jay Z sell millions of albums and stage successful tours, Dash was tossed to the curb when his former associate sold their label outright to Def Jam Recordings, then bought out Dash's stake in their Rocawear line.

"I WANT Empire. I WORKED HARD FOR THIS COMPANY."

"Piece of business advice from that Wharton education you paid so handsomely for. You pick the one who knows you're a murderer."

"I'll still be here when you're dead, Dad. I'll send a prayer down to you."

"My father is the DEVIL, and you just spread your legs for him."

"THERE WAS ALWAYS SOMETHING MISSING, DAD.

A VOID THAT I FILLED WITH DARKNESS, BUT NOW

I'M GETTING TO KNOW MY GOD. AND HE IS FILLING

THAT VOID WITH A HIGHER PURPOSE."

ANIKA CALHOUN

One of the most dynamic and dangerous people in the Empire Enterprises inner circle, Anika Calhoun was headed toward a career in either the financial world or in law after studying political science at Loyola University and earning an MBA from Harvard Business School. But when she started working for Lucious and turned out to have not only some sharp business acumen but also a great ear for a hit, she became the head of A&R at Empire.

Working so closely with Lucious leads to an intimate relationship and, in *Empire*'s first episodes, plans for marriage—but the engagement is abruptly thrown off track by the return of Cookie, who takes an immediate dislike to Anika. After Cookie starts hooking back up with Lucious, Anika retaliates by leaving Empire Enterprises to work with rival label Creedmoor. Twisting the knife further, she also sleeps with Hakeem in an attempt to use her ex-fiancé's son to tear down Empire from within.

Grace Gealey

Anika is the first television role for Grace Gealey, an Afro-Caribbean actress who studied theater at the University of South Florida and the University of California, Irvine. After graduation, she moved to New York and earned her keep acting in Off-Broadway and Broadway productions. Relocating to Chicago proved to be an auspicious decision, as she was cast in *Empire* after having been in the city for three months. Gealey was drawn to the role of Anika because she "loved how powerful and strong she was," she told *OK* magazine. "She didn't show all of her cards at once but the moments of revealing the innermost parts of herself in various scenarios were so interesting."

"Do you even know what a **DEBUTANTE** is? A **HO** who can slice your throat without **DISTURBING HER PEARLS**."

The Real-Life
ANIKA CALHOUN?

Though some say they can see traces of Rihanna (left) in Anika's character, Anika has far more business savvy than she does musical ability. Instead, Lee Daniels and his writers may have drawn a little inspiration from Sylvia Rhone (right), the former Universal Motown president who helped manage the careers of Kid Cudi, Nicki Minaj, and Akon.

THE REST

BECKY AND PORSHA

Though neither character plays a starring role in the world of *Empire*, Becky Williams and Porsha Taylor prove to be essential to the show's dramatic development. It's never stated outright, but we can assume that Becky has been with Empire Enterprises as Lucious's assistant for a while, suffering her boss's verbal abuse and random attacks with candy while also keeping him on schedule, and he trusts her enough that she's the first person he tells about his ALS diagnosis, confident that she'll keep the secret. Porsha, who's hired by Cookie as her assistant soon after her return to the Lyon family business, doesn't seem particularly good at her job, but she does keep on top of the online gossip, helping keep her boss abreast of the scandals involving Hakeem, Tiana, and the others. As a character, Porsha is pure comic relief, but considering how high-pitched and dramatic everything around her is, those kinds of laughs are necessary.

Gabourey Sidibe, who plays Becky on *Empire*, was born and raised in New York and is the daughter of an R&B singer and a cab driver. A former employee of the Fresh Air Fund, she didn't pursue acting until well into her twenties, but landed an amazing first role as the title character in Lee Daniels's critically acclaimed *Precious*. Her performance as a teen mom trying to break away from an abusive household earned her an Oscar nomination for Best Actress and a boatload of accolades, including an Independent Spirit Award, the Breakthrough Performance by an Actress Award from the National Board of Review, and an NAACP Image Award. Sidibe has since been cast in feature films like *Tower Heist*, *White*

Bird in a Blizzard, and *Life Partners* while also picking up roles in the Showtime series *The Big C* and *American Horror Story*.

As natural as she seems on camera, Ta'Rhonda Jones had never acted before netting the role of Porsha on *Empire*. The Chicagoan says she got the part after initially responding to a call for female rappers for the show. Jones wound up auditioning for the role of Tiana, but the casting agents fell in love with her style and attitude and brought her back to try out for Porsha. As she won over Daniels and the producers with her no-nonsense attitude and "ghetto fabulous" style, she was a shoo-in. In addition to her scene-stealing efforts on the show, Jones also does her own makeup and often wears her own clothes because, as she reminds anyone who interviews her, she *is* Porsha. "[She] is this carefree, live-in-the-moment type of girl," Jones told *Vulture*. "And she's gonna give it to you real. She's gonna tell no lie, and keep moving. And that's exactly how I am."

Gabourey Sidibe (top) and Ta'Rhonda Jones (bottom)

RHONDA LYON

Andre's ruthless wife often seems to be the Lady Macbeth figure goading her husband on in his efforts to take control of Empire Enterprises. At the same time, she's desperately trying to protect Andre, making sure he's taking the meds to keep his bipolar disorder in check, and proving willing to gun down anyone she sees as a real threat to his safety. Rhonda is played by veteran TV/film actress Kaitlin Doubleday, whose credits include *Catch Me If You Can*, *Hung*, and a lead role in the short-lived, GEICO-inspired sitcom *Cavemen*.

VERNON TURNER

Lucious Lyon's right-hand man at Empire Enterprises and a longtime family friend, Vernon spends much of the first season trying to help Andre take over control of the company. This ends up being his undoing as, when a fight with Andre about Jamal getting chosen as the next CEO turns physical, he is bludgeoned by Rhonda and killed. Vernon was played by Malik Yoba, the Bronx-born actor who previously had starring roles in *Cool Runnings*, *New York Undercover*, and *Why Did I Get Married?*

TIANA BROWN

One of Empire Enterprises' latest signings, this Rihanna-like singer is wooed by Hakeem and finds herself swept up in the drama surrounding the Lyon family. She winds up in even hotter water when her relationship with a woman is made public and when she starts getting professionally wooed by the people at Creedmoor. Young up-and-coming R&B artist (and friend of Taylor Swift) Serayah plays Tiana.

BUNKIE WILLIAMS

Bunkie stepped in to help Lucious and the boys when his cousin Cookie was sent to prison. He sticks with the family through it all, landing work as a driver and fixer at Empire Enterprises. But Bunkie also has a serious gambling problem, and when he's pressured to come up with the $3 million he owes, he tries to extort it from Lucious. That proves to be a fatal mistake, as Lucious kills him rather than pay. Bunkie is played on the show by Antoine McKay, a comedian and actor who can be seen in *The Weather Man*, *Prison Break*, and *Review*.

CAMILLA MARKS

This famed fashion designer, played by supermodel Naomi Campbell, is in a secret relationship with Hakeem at the start of the season, and is soon caught up in the Lyon family maelstrom.

Eventually, Lucious decides that she's a threat to his son's future and pays to have her flown back to London.

MALCOLM DEVEAUX

Hired to help Empire Enterprises deal with potential threats from the outside, Malcolm Deveaux quickly transforms the company's high-rise offices into a fortress, then tries to solidify his position by hooking up with Cookie as she fights for her piece of Empire. Malcolm is brought to life by Derek Luke, best known for his starring role in *Antwone Fisher*. He also played Sean "Puffy" Combs in the biopic *Notorious*, and had a small part in *Captain America: The First Avenger*.

OLIVIA LYON

The arrival of Jamal's ex-wife was an unexpected plot twist. Olivia shows up with who she claims is their daughter, but we soon discover that not only did Lucious pay her to marry his son to cover up the budding music star's true sexuality, he's also the real father of her child. Raven-Symoné, the former *Cosby Show* and *That's So Raven* star (and current cohost of *The View*), plays this small but memorable role.

ELLE DALLAS

The biggest surprise in *Empire*'s cast was rock star Courtney Love as Elle Dallas, a former flagship member of the record label's roster whose career has deteriorated due to drug abuse. Cookie seems to be succeeding in putting Elle on the path to redemption, but Anika sabotages her comeback by drugging Elle's drink just minutes before a major concert.

Cast member Trai Byers listens intently as writer-director Lee Daniels discusses the show.

THE
EPISODES

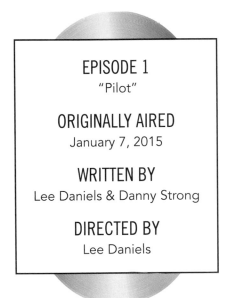

EPISODE 1
"Pilot"

ORIGINALLY AIRED
January 7, 2015

WRITTEN BY
Lee Daniels & Danny Strong

DIRECTED BY
Lee Daniels

A s Lucious Lyon announces that Empire Enterprises is about to be a publicly traded company, he also lets his three sons—Jamal, Hakeem, and Andre—know he's going to choose one of them as a successor. But then his ex-wife, Cookie, released from prison after seventeen years, demands a place at the table, as it was her $400,000 that helped launch Empire. Lucious's friend Bunkie asks for money to pay off his gambling debts, threatening to reveal dark secrets from the past if he doesn't get it. And a trip to the hospital reveals that Lucious has ALS—an incurable disease that gives him, at best, three years to live. Seeing the potential for all he has built to come crashing down, he makes the decision to cut Cookie in as a partner, and eliminates his other problem by gunning Bunkie down in cold blood.

Early in the first episode of *Empire*, after Lucious Lyon's sons learn that the patriarch and CEO of Empire Enterprises wants one of them to man up and run the company once he's gone, the middle son, Jamal, asks, "What is this? We *King Lear* now?"

Yes, Jamal. That's exactly what you are—because that's exactly what the show's cocreator Danny Strong wanted. As he told *The Atlantic* around the time of *Empire*'s premiere: "It's like *King Lear* meets hip-hop meets *Dynasty*."

And that's just what he delivered. In Shakespeare's play, an aging British monarch is slowly going insane while trying to decide which of his three daughters will get the largest share of his estate by proving that they love him the most. Here, we get a hip-hop mogul ready to take his company to the stratosphere by offering up shares of it on the New York Stock Exchange, leaving it up to his sons to demonstrate that they have the smarts and the savvy to seize the throne.

It would be heady stuff were it not for the soap opera angle that Strong and cocreator Lee Daniels injected into the mix. The Lyons are very much like the Carringtons of *Dynasty*, only instead of trading in oil, they are trying to create the next generation of pop hits (and sneakers and video games and high-end liquor). The dynamics in both families aren't too far apart either. Blake Carrington also had a homosexual son whom he worked hard to "fix" and an ex-wife who stormed into the picture, seducing or pissing off (or both) everyone around her. Strong and Daniels also work in plenty of soapy tropes with plenty of scenery-chewing histrionics (almost all of them courtesy of Cookie) and gasp-inducing dramatic reveals, including a murder at the end of the first episode that resonates throughout the season.

What sets *Empire* apart from virtually every other scripted series is its hip-hop element. Strong and Daniels worked very hard to establish the show's musical bona fides by bringing in Timbaland to help write all the music you hear in every episode and by playing up the luxurious lifestyle that the Lyons indulge in. They are talented, no doubt, but they are also living it up in style. Every inch of the *Empire* offices and the homes of the main characters is well-appointed, bordering on ostentatious. When there's music involved, like in the opening recording session where Lucious pulls an "amazing" performance out of a soul singer, or when Jamal commands the stage at a small New York club, Daniels films those scenes like a vintage Hype Williams video, all run-and-gun editing and tasteful lighting. This would be pure aspirational porn à la *Entourage* if we didn't have someone like Cookie bursting into every scene and cutting everyone down to size.

One of the inspirations for *Empire* that doesn't get talked about much is *The Lion in Winter*. James Goldman's 1966 play (better known through a 1968 film adaptation starring Peter O'Toole and Katharine Hepburn) tells the story of England's late-twelfth-century king Henry II and his wife, Eleanor of Aquitaine. Like Cookie, Eleanor has been imprisoned and returns to the kingdom with a mind toward pitting their three children against the king and each other. Of course, in the case of *Empire*, the matriarch also has more practical matters in mind, namely getting a return on the $400,000 investment she put into the company very early on. Or as she bluntly puts it, "You still owe me what's mine . . . I did seventeen hard years for that money, and I want half my company back."

Still, for all of Strong and Daniels's high-minded talk of getting inspiration from classic dramas, this is a soap opera through and through. Absolutely every one of the main characters has an agenda and reveals a conniving side that damn near illuminates many scenes with a blinking neon sign that reads, "I will stab this person in the back if it means more money for me." Cookie is the most direct, with her attacks on her ex-husband and his new flame, Anika (or as she is better known to the show's fans, Boo Boo Kitty), but cold blood runs in the Lyon family's veins. Andre, the son with no musical talent but with a head for business, decides (with some prompting by his potentially wicked wife, Rhonda) to urge his younger brothers to go to war with each other, leaving him, as he so devilishly puts it, "the last man standing." There's also Cookie's cousin Bunkie, who visits Lucious's home late at night with a gun and a threat to "light a match and . . . burn this whole bitch to the ground."

The most cold-blooded, of course, is Lucious himself. Here is a guy who was more than willing to send his wife up the river for his sins, then divorce her while she was on the inside. A guy who is happy to have his three children sing for their supper while they climb all over one another to prove their worthiness to him. A guy who would shoot his lifelong friend in the face lest it threaten his status as a potential billionaire (and would do so with the groan-worthy line, "I never let anything come between a friendship . . . except a bullet").

The lack of sympathetic characters is one of the things that can make soap operas so much fun, though. The closest we get to someone we can root for is Jamal, the artistically conflicted and sexually closeted artist with the musical Midas touch. His father's issues with his homosexuality are the one piece of *Empire* that is literally and figuratively rooted in real-world concerns.

Despite the increased awareness and acceptance of gay rights in today's world, anyone who identifies as LGBT is still likely to be stigmatized within the hip-hop and African American communities. Even Jamal's mother refers to him throughout the hour as a queen, a sissy, and a faggot. He may be the true artiste of the family, but he's also holding himself back from the spotlight, because being in it would force him to open up about his homosexuality.

Considering one of the most talked-about scenes in the first episode, can anyone blame him? It was a moment that was completely pulled from the pages of Lee Daniels's own life. The Academy Award–nominated filmmaker was actually shoved into a garbage can by his angry father just for trying on a pair of his mother's high heels. As overblown as that scene seemed when played out on-screen, it obviously meant a lot to Daniels to put it in the show. As Terrence Howard told *Deadline*, when they were filming it the director "had to look away because he was in tears, because he was facing it."

Outside of that nod to his past and his decision to name some of the characters after people from his childhood growing up in Philadelphia, Daniels knows that he's making a show that borders on pure camp. Otherwise he wouldn't have hired actors who go right to the edge of overacting and move from deeply hurt to raging fury in a heartbeat. What comes through loud and clear in this first episode is that Strong and Daniels know that they are making a high-pitched drama that's meant to leave us cackling and hollering at the screen with each of Cookie's outrageous outfits and every instance of her even more outrageous dialogue. *Empire* is a show that wanted your full attention from the jump, while also leaving plenty of room for viewers with their locked-and-loaded smartphones to comment on each episode in real time. You won't get *that* with no Shakespeare play.

Terrence Howard and Lee Daniels share a relaxed moment.

★ LUCIOUS LYON vs. KING LEAR ★

So if *Empire* is supposed to be like a hip-hop version of *King Lear*, how does the embattled CEO of a major media company stack up against an aging English king? Lear isn't the best role model for Lucious or, well, anyone in a position of power. Not only does he make his daughters vie for his affection with the promise of wealth to the one who most convincingly expresses her love, he completely disowns the daughter who wants no part of the game. This ends up being the undoing of his family (spoiler alert!): By the end of the play, his daughters are all dead and the grief ends up killing him, too. Unless *Empire* is desperate for a ratings boost in a later season, all four of the main characters aren't likely to go out in one fell swoop like that. But Lucious is just crazy enough that he seems willing to let his sons tear each other apart as they try to become his successor. What better way to remind them that no matter how close they get to taking the crown, he's still very much in control?

Bryshere Y. Gray and Jussie Smollet perform together at the Billboard Music Awards.

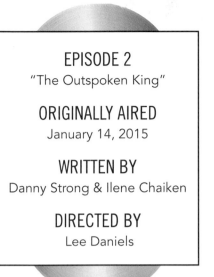

EPISODE 2
"The Outspoken King"

ORIGINALLY AIRED
January 14, 2015

WRITTEN BY
Danny Strong & Ilene Chaiken

DIRECTED BY
Lee Daniels

With Empire Enterprises' impending IPO all over the news, Lucious turns his attention to his new club, Leviticus. Cookie insists that Jamal perform at the opening, an idea Lucious rebuffs, saying he doesn't want Leviticus to get "branded as a homosexual club." Instead, he wants to use opening night to introduce his son Hakeem to the world with a spotlight performance. As he challenges his staff to find the right support act for the show, he gets an opportunity handed to him with the news of a gunman shooting up a suburban shopping mall and claiming he was inspired by the lyrics of Empire artist Kidd Fo-Fo (played by Kristopher Lofton).

The police turn up Bunkie's body, and Lucious breaks the news to the family and demands vengeance. Reacting to the news, Hakeem gets drunk in an upscale bar and is caught on video pissing on the carpet and calling Barack Obama a "sellout." With Cookie's help, Jamal decides to come out of the closet as part of a publicity stunt meant to divert attention away from Leviticus. Once Lucious learns of this, he tells his son that if he does so, he will receive no more financial *support. Conflicted, Jamal doesn't show up for the big press conference Cookie has arranged, but does get a big moment in the spotlight when he performs with Hakeem at Leviticus, much to the surprise of their father. Before the night's out, Cookie is confronted by the FBI, who insist that she has to testify in front of a grand jury or risk being sent back to prison.*

Just how callous and devious is Lucious? So much so that when he tells his family about Bunkie's murder, he does so with tears in his eyes, insisting that he will find out who did this to his beloved friend. It's a masterful performance that convinces everyone in the room. And it's the kind of acting that Lucious has probably had to do his entire life. He has almost certainly killed other people when he was a drug dealer, and he can't even own up to the fact that his previous line of work tore apart his community and ruined the lives of many of his customers. Instead, he sticks to the story he tells to the Fox News–like pundit who interviews him about the Kidd Fo-Fo controversy: "You either sold drugs or your family goes hungry."

Lucious is, in that way, very much like other morally bankrupt TV protagonists, such as Tony Soprano or Walter White. He revels in the wealth he has acquired and the power that comes with it. Anything that challenges his authority or threatens his bank account has to be stamped out before it grows into a full-bore insurrection. But because *Empire* is a network drama, the writers can't delve as deeply into the gray areas of their main character's ethics in the ways cable shows like *The Sopranos* or *Breaking Bad* did every week.

Nor can the series explore some of the issues that this episode skims past. The fictional news commentator Kelly McGann spouts some of the same rhetoric heard from real-life pundits like Bill O'Reilly, blaming rap lyrics for many of America's ills. There was also a chance to comment on how smartphones and viral videos have changed the game for many of today's less mature musicians, when Hakeem was caught being an asshole at a bar (mirroring a real-life Justin Bieber incident), but that slipped right through the show's fingers. It does get a few jabs in at modern pop stars, like when Kidd Fo-Fo compares himself unironically to Gandhi and doesn't have a clue who Diana Ross is. Beyond those critical grace notes, however, *Empire* sticks to its soap opera roots, presenting everything in big, broad strokes with zero ambiguity.

That's why it's hard to swallow Lucious's big moment of moral clarity, when he drops Kidd Fo-Fo from the label after the rapper repeatedly insults Cookie. Nor is it easy to feel any sympathy for Cookie over being treated so poorly, not after we've just seen her snarling and snapping and calling her ex-husband nothing short of a sellout.

That's what makes *Empire* a true soap opera. The writers brushed aside continuity from week to week, drawing the shortest line between two scenes, as long as the connections were dramatically convenient. It sometimes felt as though the show was trying to reinvent itself each week, as plotlines and characters disappeared with an almost callous disregard. If characters could help move the story along, and help Fox score more downloads of that episode, great. Once that was done, they had to get the hell out of the way.

Just two episodes in, the writers were free to continue establishing the series' core qualities; with "The Outspoken King," it was the sex appeal they tried to bake into the mix. They got about as risqué as any midweek primetime show could, with plenty of scantily clad women (many of them extras dancing in a rehearsal for a video by Tiana, a new Empire signing), and the main female characters using their bodies to their full advantage to gain control of a situation.

As Andre reveals that he's been playing fast and loose with the meds controlling his bipolar disorder, Rhonda convinces him to make another doctor's appointment by tying what is essentially a bib around her neck and dropping to her knees in front of her husband to provide added . . . incentive . . . to the negotiations. Even more to the point is Anika parading around her house in black lingerie as a way to both steal Lucious's attention away from a conversation he is having with Cookie and to annoy the unwanted visitor. A catty move, but a damn effective one.

More than anything else in this episode, everyone seems still to be reeling from the news that Lucious will be handing control of Empire Enterprises over to one of his sons. Andre, Jamal, and Hakeem seem to flap around the scenes like manic birds, trying to figure out how best to fluff their feathers up for their father's attention and approval. Like many patriarchal figures, Lucious wields a huge influence and power over his sons, even though they are all grown men. No one can really stand up to him. Not Hakeem, when he tries gamely to rhyme over his dad's whack beat. And definitely not Andre, who is trying to remind Lucious of that sweet little boy who used to show up at the office wearing a suit and try to help with executive matters. The only one who comes close to pushing back is Jamal, but once he realizes how many of his creature comforts he will be giving up as a result, he folds.

That's why Cookie is such an important presence on the show. She's strong enough to call Lucious on his bullshit, knowing that it's going to have an effect on him. That's also what makes her scenes with Anika so delicious. They both want to have control of Lucious's puppet strings, and all he can do is sit there and grimace while the two trade barbs. For instance, Cookie tells him to "drop this yella bitch," to which Anika responds: "Yeah, he probably will when I'm your age. Except by then, he'll probably be . . . 110?" Okay, so it's not the sharpest retort, but the point is loud and clear: She's got Cookie's man now and she's not gonna let him go without something nasty happening as a result.

★ LUCIOUS LYON vs. GENGHIS KHAN ★

While Lucious isn't going to try to conquer the known world via military campaigns anytime soon, the fictional hip-hop icon's life does have some interesting similarities to that of the Mongol leader who ruled over the second-largest empire in history. Both men were notoriously promiscuous, with illegitimate children left behind in their wake, while they maintained a strict line of succession that centered on three potential male heirs. And just as Genghis Khan managed to connect previously separate worlds, thereby insuring a cross-pollination of cultural ideas, so too has Lucious helped bring major players in R&B, hip-hop, and pop together with exciting results. Oh, and they're both stone-cold killers.

The battles between Cookie (Taraji P. Henson) and Anika (Grace Gealey)—over Empire, and over Lucious—are one of the show's biggest dramatic hooks.

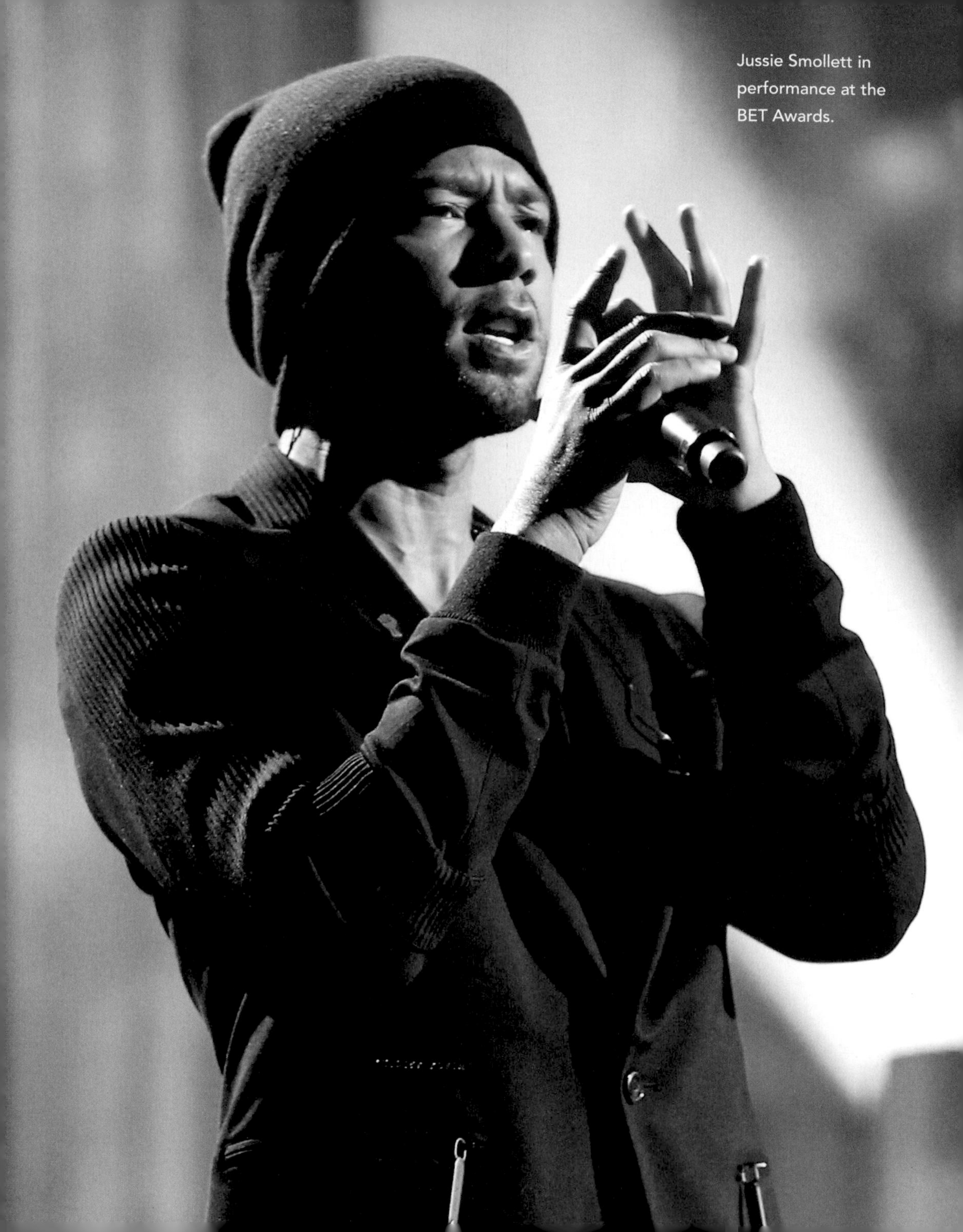

Jussie Smollett in performance at the BET Awards.

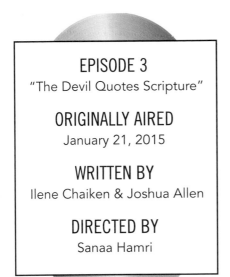

EPISODE 3
"The Devil Quotes Scripture"

ORIGINALLY AIRED
January 21, 2015

WRITTEN BY
Ilene Chaiken & Joshua Allen

DIRECTED BY
Sanaa Hamri

While preparing for Bunkie's funeral, Lucious learns that Kidd Fo-Fo has signed with rival label Creedmoor Records and directs his A&R team to dig up every bit of dirt they can on CEO Billy Beretti. Meanwhile, Cookie tries to find the perfect "breakout hit" for Jamal, eventually contacting an old associate of the label, Puma (played by Cuba Gooding Jr.). At first her old friend rebuffs her, but finally decides to give her a song: a tune he wrote about Cookie that Lucious had rejected years before. As the police grill the witness to Bunkie's murder— a homeless alcoholic amputee named Ol' Salty—Andre uses his influence (aka sexing up the deputy mayor) to get information about the investigation. Anika reveals that she hired a private investigator to tail Cookie, and has pictures of her talking to an FBI agent. The fed in question, though, convinces Lucious she's Cookie's parole officer. Everything comes to a head at a dinner party at Lucious's house. There, Andre gamely tries to get into Hakeem's head about how their other brother is the true talent of the family, and Jamal plays his arrangement of Puma's song for everyone. It turns out Lucious already owns the song, and he decides to take it back and hand it to another artist. Later on, Lucious shows up at Jamal's apartment, and the two have a nasty argument that culminates in the younger Lyon deciding to reject his father's financial support and make a play for the control of Empire Enterprises.

For all the women and LGBT rappers whose careers are thriving today, hip-hop is still considered the domain of straight men. That's why almost all the figures in that world who may have provided inspiration for the character of Lucious Lyon (such as Suge Knight, Puff Daddy, and Jay Z) are larger-than-life braggarts who demand attention, demand that their ideas be respected. That's why Cookie's comment that she's supporting Jamal because she wants to show "that a faggot really can run this company" has much more oomph than Lucious telling his sons, "In order for this company to survive, I want one of you negroes to man up and lead it." Even though his talented son may be considered a "sissy," he's supposed to push that aside and act like a *boss*.

Little does Lucious know that all the years of abuse and confrontations with Jamal were lighting a fire in the young man's belly that, in this episode, become a bonfire. The final conversation between the two in this installment is filled with jibes and jabs that the patriarch has likely been tossing at his son for decades. He insists that if Jamal doesn't "toughen up, these streets will eat your ass alive," and tells him he didn't raise him to "become somebody's bitch." It is horrible to listen to, but it adds up to the most honest scene in the show to this point.

Lucious's emphasis on this kind of masculinity proves to have left some interesting psychological scars on his other sons as well. Though Andre shows himself capable of exhibiting some of his father's more animalistic tendencies when he tosses around the deputy mayor to get information out of her (and then reenacts the scene later with Rhonda), his efforts to bring that into his strong-arming of Hakeem just comes off as mean and uncomfortable. He can't seem to push the same buttons when it is another man. Hakeem, on the other hand, turns out to have quite an Oedipus complex. Although he's dating Tiana, he's got a side piece in the form of Camilla, a middle-aged British fashion designer (played by Naomi Campbell) who insists on being called Mommy during their more intimate encounters. It would be creepy if it didn't make so much sense considering the household Hakeem grew up in.

Writers Ilene Chaiken and Joshua Allen drive this point about masculinity home even further with Lucious. Early in the episode, he deals with the pushy manager of one of his starlets by inviting him into his trailer and beating on him. He's also livid when he learns his former mentor and current rival, Billy Beretti, has snapped up Kidd Fo-Fo, only because the Creedmoor CEO is "controlling the story." The deepest moment, though, happens outside Bunkie's funeral when Lucious happens upon a young boy in tears and tells him, "You know, men don't cry." The fact that not two minutes later we see the grown man weeping openly during the funeral proves to be a nice bit of irony for the show.

There is also a bit of contrast to Lucious's chest-pounding braggadocio in this episode, too, in the form of Puma. By the time Cookie tracks him down, she finds that he's left the music industry behind completely and is now running a horse farm that doubles as a camp for troubled kids. The unwritten question that Chaiken and Allen seem to be asking is, "Who's the bigger man: the swaggering, quick-with-a-crowbar hip-hop impresario or a humble man trying to positively impact the lives of young people at a handsomely appointed ranch?" After watching Lucious treat his sons like pawns in his strange game and trying to wriggle out of the grip of the police, I'm leaning toward Puma.

Speaking of which, the small subplot of Cookie trying to find the right song for Jamal feels like an understated commentary on the current sound of R&B. The one candidate we hear is a supremely dumb party anthem, infused with EDM beats and awful lyrics about popping bottles and hitting the dance floor. She then tries to coax something from two spacey Norwegian hit makers who happen to be in the building. It seems to be a nod to Stargate, the songwriting/production team that helped create "Irreplaceable" for Beyoncé and Rihanna's "Diamonds" and helped turn many other African American artists into icy Nordic pop divas. That style is far removed from where Cookie sits, no matter how desperately she wants to give her son a hit. The song from Puma may sound old-school but to her ears, it's the perfect combination of pop smarts and honest urban aesthetic.

While this episode reserves its smartest writing for the subtle look at how masculinity is viewed in hip-hop and within the African American community, it falls flat when it comes to the big story arcs. Lucious's symptoms of ALS start popping up at one point, but no one trusts that the viewers will be able to pick up on that, so they have him self-narrate ("Doctor said I wouldn't have these cramps yet"). And when the writers try to deepen the drama of a potential witness to Bunkie's murder, every scene feels like an afterthought. You had a paranoid schizophrenic named Ol' Salty, living under a bridge by the river, spouting Bible verses as he looks all wild-eyed and shifty—the character is a simplistic turnkey, created solely to put the sliver of suspicion in the cops' mind that Lucious might be behind the murder. Even the seduction scene between Andre and the deputy mayor just feels icky and weird.

"The Devil Quotes Scripture" gives the deep impression of a series that is still trying to find its way. When it does find steady footing, especially during the tense dinner party at Lucious's home and the emotional showdown between Jamal and his dad, there is a feeling that *Empire* is capable of moving beyond its soapy, campy elements—at least far enough to make those more overheated moments feel less glaring. The writers, though, seem committed to the shakiness and ludicrousness of the shows that inspired it, which require corny scenes like Jamal declaring darkly into the camera, "I'm going after his empire . . . and I'm gonna take it!" Moments like that threaten to turn *Empire* into empty-calorie TV: the kind of show you can't resist watching, but feel super guilty about afterward.

GUEST STAR

CUBA GOODING JR.

One of the most surprising additions to the show is Cuba Gooding Jr. popping up as former Empire Enterprises songwriter Puma. This appearance represents an upswing in activity for this actor, who recently won acclaim for his self-parodying performance on Comedy Central's *Big Time in Hollywood, FL*, and his upcoming role as O.J. Simpson in the series *American Crime Story*. Not that he's been in hiding, mind you. Since winning an Oscar for playing the over-the-top football star Rod Tidwell in *Jerry Maguire*, Gooding Jr. has appeared in dozens of films and TV series, including in Lee Daniels's *The Butler* and in a starring role as famed neurosurgeon Ben Carson in the TV movie *Gifted Hands*.

GLADYS KNIGHT

The Empress of Soul, Knight makes her big appearance in this episode singing haunting gospel tunes to the congregation of mourners at Bunkie's funeral. The Atlanta-born, Grammy-winning singer rose to fame in the late '60s with her group Gladys Knight and the Pips, scoring top 10 hits like "Midnight Train to Georgia" and "You're the Best Thing that Ever Happened to Me." Since splitting with the group in 1987, Knight has sustained a steady solo career while also taking acting roles in films like Tyler Perry's *I Can Do Bad All by Myself* and the Harrison Ford–starring cop drama *Hollywood Homicide*.

Jussie Smollett's fame skyrocketed over the course of *Empire's* first season, as the character of Jamal became a favorite with the show's fans.

★ LUCIOUS LYON vs. CYRUS THE GREAT ★

While Cyrus the Great won many significant military victories in his thirty-year reign over the Persian Empire, he is best remembered for the good that he brought to his vast domain. According to historical records, Cyrus helped create one of the first postal services, allowed all the people under his rule to practice whatever religion they chose, installed roadways connecting the various regions of his kingdom, and helped the citizens displaced by his predecessor return to their home countries. Lucious doesn't have nearly as many issues to worry about, but he could sure learn some lessons in diplomacy from this ancient ruler.

Serayah & Bryshere Y. Gray in a duet performance at the Billboard Music Awards.

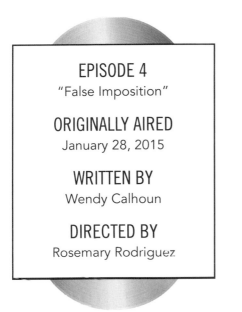

EPISODE 4
"False Imposition"

ORIGINALLY AIRED
January 28, 2015

WRITTEN BY
Wendy Calhoun

DIRECTED BY
Rosemary Rodriguez

Titan, a famous rapper signed to Creedmoor Records, gets into a shootout with a rival after one of his shows, leading to his arrest and incarceration. With this news, and a chance to hit back at Billy Beretti, Lucious, Anika, and Cookie all get in the hunt, reaching out to Titan's managers and his mother. This puts added pressure on Hakeem to deliver on his next track. Luckily, Tiana comes along with the demo for a new song, and at Cookie's urging the two perform it as a duet. Jamal, meanwhile, is now living in a sketchy apartment in Bushwick, Brooklyn, where he struggles to find inspiration. In the midst of this, the police come calling at Empire Enterprises' offices, looking for Lucious to provide an alibi for the night Bunkie was killed. Andre helps him out, claiming they were watching a boxing match together. And Lucious finally opens up to Anika about his ALS diagnosis.

"False Imposition" is perhaps the most hip-hop-centric episode of *Empire*'s first season. The story arcs of Lucious's illness, Bunkie's murder, and the three sons gaming to take control of Empire barely move forward, as the show takes a step back into one of hip-hop's most troubled periods.

The 1990s were an amazing time for hip-hop, producing world-beating artists like A Tribe Called Quest, 2Pac, Dr. Dre, and the Pharcyde, cementing the music as the sound of youth culture. But the decade was also marked by intense beefs between rappers and labels. At best, the disputes were mere wars of words, with artists throwing verbal shots at one another in the press and on their albums. At worst, they traded gunfire—and some artists didn't make it out alive.

Where *Empire* sometimes keeps the parallels between its fictional characters and real life obscure, in this episode, the links are much clearer. The rivalry between Lucious and Beretti is a much tamer version of the nasty feud between Suge Knight's Death Row Records and Puff Daddy's Bad Boy Entertainment. But not too tame: mirroring the real drive-by shooting that took place when Tha Dogg Pound was filming the video for "New York, New York"—their diss of the Empire State—when Anika and Lucious sit down to try and pull Titan away from Creedmoor, someone cruises by and starts spraying bullets at them.

Some of the accusations Lucious levels at Beretti during their brief sit-down and mutually threatening session at Leviticus—primarily that the Creedmoor head had added his name to the writing credits on Lucious's early albums, thus snagging a piece of the royalties—are the sorts of shady practices likely still going on in the industry today. One notorious story involves Knight allegedly dangling Vanilla Ice out of a window to urge the rapper to add the name of a Death Row artist to the writing credits for "Ice Ice Baby." Even Beyoncé has allegedly tried her hand at this, sticking her name in the credits of "I Miss You," a song on her album 4 that, according to songwriter Frank Ocean, she didn't add anything to. (This is hardly limited to the hip-hop community, though, nor is it a recent phenomenon. Colonel Tom Parker could be relentless in his efforts to get Elvis Presley, whom he managed, a cowriting credit on songs he recorded.)

There is also a little nod to jailed rappers recording tracks while behind bars. Once Lucious finally convinces Titan to join Empire, he hands the rhymer a smartphone to record new music onto. This practice has been going since the '90s (at least), with artists big and small using their phone privileges to call up and record new verses over the line. Some prisons have even started allowing inmates to build recording studios within their walls, something that serves as a vital creative outlet and a way to learn a marketable skill for when they are released.

Another aspect of the hip-hop industry (though, again, not unique to that world) reflected in this episode is the tendency for everyone involved in the business to constantly look for the means to boost their status and cut someone else down to size. That can, of course, be fun to watch when Cookie and Anika are at each other's throats, but it can also reveal the greediest side of the industry. Even after Tiana walks in on Hakeem in a bubble bath with Camilla and storms out, for example, she brushes it aside because she doesn't want to jeopardize her piece of the spotlight during their performance at the Teen Choice Awards nomination party.

The only unsullied artist in the show is Jamal. Free of his father's money, he's now living in a shithole apartment and trying to tease out some new music. He's so committed to his independence and his integrity that he returns a check that Empire sends him for backing up Hakeem at the Leviticus opening. What does he get for all that virtuousness? Writer's block. At the very end of the episode, we see Jamal step outside and start to tease some inspiration out of the sounds of the street (with a cute little nod to Michael Jackson's "Black or White" video thrown in for good measure). If he were a real person, he would be the artist refusing a Spotify or Tidal deal, and releasing his music only through Bandcamp. And he'd likely score a 9.7 review on Pitchfork.

Empire also gives viewers the most idyllic version of creativity in this episode, imagining a world where the kernel of an idea, like the one Tiana has for her song "Dangerous," can turn into an absolute banger of a track with Hakeem's interjections and their crazy chemistry. Or where Jamal can rattle some chains and bang out a beat on a dumpster and potentially hit upon his next big single. Those eureka breakthroughs, and moments where artists can overcome everything to find common ground and produce something amazing together, are common fantasies of how the creative process works.

Ultimately, it's that romanticizing tendency that makes this episode's spin on hip-hop feuds somewhat disappointing. For all the amazing music that came out of the '90s scene, we were also left with the deaths of 2Pac, The Notorious B.I.G., and many others. *Empire* acknowledges the violence of that era but softens the consequences for the sake of entertainment.

GUEST STAR

Judd Nelson

If you grew up in the 1980s, Judd Nelson, along with the rest of the young actors known as the Brat Pack, was inescapable. After his breakout role as the burnout John Bender in *The Breakfast Club*, Nelson went on to star in *St. Elmo's Fire*, the courtroom dramedy *From the Hip*, and the psychological thriller *Relentless*. Over the years, he has stayed busy working on movies big and small, including a starring role in Brooke Shields's '90s sitcom *Suddenly Susan*. Nelson's role in *Empire* is one of his most high-profile appearances in recent years, but it's also a bit of a throwback, as his character's name is an homage to Nick Peretti, the role he had in the hip-hop-infused crime thriller *New Jack City*.

Taraji P. Henson strongly encouraged *Empire* co-creator Lee Daniels to cast Terrence Howard as Lucious; the two actors first starred together in the 2005 film *Hustle & Flow*.

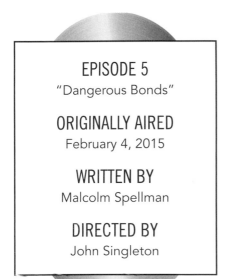

EPISODE 5
"Dangerous Bonds"

ORIGINALLY AIRED
February 4, 2015

WRITTEN BY
Malcolm Spellman

DIRECTED BY
John Singleton

*L*ucious proposes to Anika, who instantly agrees. Both decide to slowly introduce the news to their respective families because they know they're going to face obstacles. Hakeem gets ready to release his new song and video, "Drip Drop." At the same time, Jamal has gone into a studio in a sketchy neighborhood to work on his brand-new song. Andre and Rhonda conspire to drive Hakeem crazy and drive a wedge between the other brothers. First they release footage of his girlfriend, Tiana, fooling around with another woman, then convince some of his entourage to go rob the studio where Jamal is working, culminating in a tense standoff between the two younger Lyons. Cookie testifies before a grand jury, implicating a former associate, Frank Gathers, in the murder of an undercover FBI agent. Later, she panics when a red rose—the symbol Gathers used on all his drug packages—is left on her doorstep. Through her sister, she finds out it was likely the work of another Gathers associate, so she hires an old friend to "handle" the situation. Later, though, she learns the rose was left by Lucious in honor of the anniversary of their marriage. She tries to call off the hit—but it's too late.

With "Dangerous Bonds," *Empire* achieved the perfect balance of its commercial intentions: finding a way to promote new music from Yazz the Greatest and Jussie Smollett, while ratcheting up the drama with gasp-inducing cliffhangers, gunplay, lesbian affairs, and lots of sharp-tongued commentary from Cookie.

Mostly, the episode returns the show to its core premise: a family tearing itself apart out of pride, greed, and chest-puffing masculinity. Even the so-called "sissy" of the show, Jamal, proves himself to be as tough as can be, standing up to a man wielding a gun and punching Hakeem in the gut as the two square off about the robbery and their creative rivalry. And smiling through it all is Andre, the puppet master of this little drama, who is using his leverage and business smarts to charm Lucious even as he's pitting his younger brothers against each other.

We also get a deeper look into the lives of the two women vying for Lucious's attention. We learn that Anika was once a gifted musician who was Juilliard-bound before she decided to leave it all to work behind the scenes in the record industry. We also get a glimpse into the unsteady relationship between her and Lucious as her mother reminds her of those nights when she would come back home in tears because of "all those other women." Anika assures her mom her future husband has changed, but it isn't long before we see him in full seduction mode with Cookie, not to mention messing about with a lingerie-clad model on the set of Hakeem's video.

Cookie's backstory only serves to reveal what a miracle it is she and her kids got out of Philadelphia alive. It also shows us the lengths she will go to in order to survive. She hardly blinks or even looks conflicted over ordering a hit on one of Frank Gathers's associates—and even though it turns out to be unnecessary, she probably won't lose much sleep over the fact that she paid $5,000 to have someone killed. That's just the law of the streets.

Like Jamal and Hakeem, Cookie provides a perfect contrast to the life her ex-husband has created. She likes the life of luxury her career in the music industry is providing for her, but she's also not far removed from her roots as a drug dealer fighting for her life on the crime-ridden streets of Philadelphia. She brings a lot of that steely attitude and boldness to her interactions in the boardroom and high-rise offices of Empire Enterprises. That's why she feels comfortable bursting into any situation that she feels she deserves to be a part of.

Lucious, on the other hand, has adapted to the moneyed lifestyle a little too well. Watching him saunter through this world is like listening to Jay Z rapping about his expensive taste in art and the struggle of being one of the most famous people in the world on *Magna Carta Holy Grail*, all traces of the man who sold crack on the streets of Brooklyn erased. Like Mr. Beyoncé, Lucious may be the product of growing up on tough streets, but he's miles away from that world, mentally and physically now. He has fully embraced the tailored suits, and he loves being able to buy a huge engagement ring for Anika instead of having to steal a rose to give to Cookie on their anniversary way back when. But he still has to hustle—this time to convince his future father-in-law to sign off on a false document stating that he is in good health. Though Anika's dad calls Lucious a "thug," he comes around when he is told that if the IPO goes through, it will make his daughter a billionaire.

That same dynamic is playing out between Hakeem and Jamal. The smartest thing director John Singleton and writer Malcolm Spellman do is bounce between the video shoot for "Drip Drop" and the recording session for "Keep Your Money." Jamal's song is a little on the nose about his rejection of his father's support, but this show doesn't have time for subtlety. So we get to see the stark contrast between the tiny, graffitied studio that Jamal is working in and the CGI technology and scantily clad ladies who Hakeem is working with.

That disparity also comes out in how the two men think about their music. Hakeem's concern is pushing aside Kendrick Lamar, J. Cole, and Drake for his chance in the spotlight, while also "changing the game" in the manner of 50 Cent's lucrative endorsement deal with Vitamin Water and Dr. Dre's incredibly successful line of Beats headphones. As he says, "I want to show them I'm the king." Jamal, though, may actually be telling the truth when he says that it's all about the music.

The producers of *Empire* do a great job of emphasizing just how connected Jamal and Hakeem are, no matter how frayed their relationship is. Listen closely during those scenes where the men are working on their respective videos and recording sessions, and you'll notice that the individual songs actually mix together really well. At one point toward the end of the episode, they even move between a screening of the "Drip Drop" clip and Jamal playing the finished version of "Keep Your Money" for his mom, and you might forget where one ends and the other begins. As far apart as Jamal and Hakeem are with regard to their views on artistic success, they still come from the same gene pool.

LUCIOUS LYON vs. ALEXANDER THE GREAT

Like our friend Lucious, Alexander the Great accomplished a lot at a very young age. The Greek ruler was named king of Macedonia at age twenty, after his father passed away, and he spent the next ten years waging military campaigns. By the end, he was in control of much of the known world. It's a far cry from slinging cocaine on the streets and building a huge corporation, but both men knew how to use money to fix problems and kill or humiliate anyone who wasn't supporting their reigns. And both Lucious and Alexander loved stamping their names on things as a way of securing a legacy that will stand long after they're gone.

Anthony Hamilton

Anika's favorite recording artist, this crooner helps set the romantic mood for Lucious to pop the question. In real life, Hamilton has had a varied career. He's mostly known for his collaboration with various hip-hop artists, including his Grammy-nominated turn on the Nappy Roots song "Po' Folks" and on Nas's #1 album *Life Is Good*. His own albums have found great success as well, as evidenced by the sale of more than a million copies of his second album, *Comin' from Where I'm From*, which also earned him three more Grammy nods.

After being prominently featured in musical performances throughout the season, Jussie Smollett signed his own recording contract with Columbia Records.

EPISODE 6
"Out, Damned Spot"

ORIGINALLY AIRED
February 11, 2015

WRITTEN BY
Eric Haywood

DIRECTED BY
Michael Engler

T hinking the rose Lucious gave her was flirtatious, Cookie gets dressed up in a seductive outfit to meet her ex at a restaurant. To her surprise, she learns it was part of the announcement of Lucious and Anika's engagement. Lucious's right-hand man, Vernon, finds out his boss killed Bunkie and leaps into action. He confronts Andre about the alibi he provided for his dad, sets up another man to confess to the murder, and beefs up the security at Empire Enterprises with the hire of Malcolm Deveaux. With the IPO looming, the label decides to start cutting dead weight from the roster, including former star Elle Dallas (played by Courtney Love). Cookie balks at this suggestion and decides to take Dallas on as a new client. She also finds time to help get buzz going about Jamal's new track. The attention, though, starts to put pressure on his relationship with Michael, which gets amplified when, during a satellite radio interview, Jamal dismisses the idea of him having a special someone in his life. Just when everyone starts to get comfortable, a surprise visitor stops by Empire's offices: Olivia, a friend of the family who has brought along Lola, who she claims is Jamal's five-year-old daughter.

The title of Episode 6, "Out, Damned Spot," comes from Shakespeare's *Macbeth*; it's a famous line of Lady Macbeth's from late in the play when, tormented by guilt concerning her husband's murder of King Duncan (and her role in goading him to it), she's convinced that she has blood on her hand that she needs to scrub clean.

The obvious connection to this episode is Vernon's efforts to wash away Lucious's murder of Bunkie, and the slight guilt that his boss might still be feeling about shooting a lifelong friend in the face. But it's also an example of *Empire*'s lofty intentions to bring a little Elizabethan drama to the world of hip-hop and serve it up to a prime-time viewing audience. Try as the writers and producers might, though, they really can't elevate their subject matter beyond the level of their other inspiration: '80s prime-time soap operas like *Dynasty* and *Dallas*. Then again, considering that those soapy elements might well be what drew viewers in, *Empire* could just be one of the most self-aware shows around—delivering overcooked TV drama and playing it to the hilt.

To that end, this episode delivers the goods, big time, and sets up conflicts and concerns that carry through the rest of the season. The biggest one is the relationship between Vernon and Andre. They both perform essential roles in the Empire Enterprises machine: a fixer willing to overstep legal bounds to protect his friend and employer, and a financial wizard trying to keep the company solvent as it roars toward billion-dollar status. Like it or not, if they are going to rise to the top, they need each other. Which is exactly why Vernon freaks out and attacks Andre for daring to provide an alibi for his father without even knowing the charges. Covering up Lucious's crimes is only going to put their potential takeover in danger. But it does give us a chance to see Vernon in action; after residing in the background of most everything Empire-related so far, he's positioning himself to take a lead role in the company's future—where he'll be ready to shove Lucious out the door, or off a cliff, when the time comes.

The other key theme for this episode comes from Cookie, who warns Jamal's boyfriend, Michael, that "fame changes people." That's true of nearly everyone in the show but especially of up-and-coming R&B singer Jamal. For all of his lecturing about how it's all about the music for him, Jamal is basking in the glow of all the attention, to the point that he's willing to sacrifice time with Michael to do an interview on satellite radio, where he freezes when the opportunity to come out arises. You can almost hear his internal monologue as he tries to figure out what the right move is—and when he chooses to stay in the spotlight, it comes at a personal cost.

Another figure whose life has been upended by success is Elle Dallas, a former recording star for Empire Enterprises played by Courtney Love. Beyond the stunt casting itself, bringing Love in to play a singer whose career has seen better days is a fairly genius move. Though she insisted to *TV Guide* that she is "not playing myself" but rather channeling the "mindset of a real diva" like Mariah Carey or Madonna, it's not hard to see how this part was written to reflect bits of Love's own life, including Elle's drug addiction and her insistence on wearing ostentatious outfits and makeup to hide the effects of aging.

Elle has also let the idea of fame go to her head in the worst way. She may have actually been the person who kept the lights on at Empire for a long time, but because it's been years since she's made any kind of impact, she can't make the demands on Lucious that she once did, including getting her a big-time producer like Timbaland to work with. She stomps and storms around the studio trying to get her way even though she can barely sing on key. Though the results weren't *that* great, it was still impressive to see Cookie literally dress Elle down, forcing her to remove all the artifice and reach for something beyond the glamour in her performance. (You only wish someone would do the same for Courtney Love herself.)

Of course, celebrity has affected Lucious the most. In his most telling verbal slip, he insists to Vernon that he had to commit the murder because Bunkie was threatening "everything that I built . . . everything *we* built." No matter how often he's reminded that his ex-wife's money helped start the company, or that he has hundreds of people making the little decisions that keep his empire afloat, it is, as Drake would put it, "all me." He has the money to take care of anything, even a possible murder charge, and no hesitation about using it. Need experimental drugs smuggled in from Russia to help combat his ALS? No problem. Want to prove to the world that your love for your fiancée is legitimate? Put a gigantic rock on her hand. It would be disgusting if he weren't such a compelling character.

That could be a huge component of why people kept flocking to *Empire* in unprecedented numbers week after week during the first season. Unlike *Entourage*, where there were no consequences or bills for the lavish, outlandish behavior, viewers knew that Lucious would suffer a literal or metaphorical fall at some point before the first season came to an end. All of his strong-arm tactics and carelessness with the hearts of the people closest to him had to be building up to a comeuppance he deserved and surely needed—and when it came, it was going to be so satisfying to watch.

★ LUCIOUS LYON VS. MACBETH ★

Though Lee Daniels and Danny Strong haven't cited Shakespeare's Scottish Play as a direct inspiration for *Empire*, the
main characters could, at times, trade places without upsetting
the mood of either drama. Both Lucious and Macbeth have
been corrupted by their appetite for power, and prove willing
to do whatever it takes to get it and hold on to it, including the
murder of those closest to them. And they pay no attention to
whom they're hurting or driving mad as a result of their blind
ambition. Of course, Lucious has yet to reveal that he received
any prophecies from a trio of witches about his rise to power,
but with all that bullshit he spews to get his way, I wouldn't put
it past him.

Courtney Love

This alternative rock icon came to the world's attention not only through the visceral, wrenching music she recorded with her band Hole but as the wife of the biggest rock star of the 1990s, Kurt Cobain. Following her husband's suicide, Love has stayed in the spotlight, less for her music than for her issues with substance abuse and her very public squabbles with other musicians—and even her daughter. In recent years she has found some balance with steady acting work in shows like *Sons of Anarchy* and *Revenge*, as well as being invited to be the opening act for Lana Del Rey's summer arena tour.

Bryshere Y. Gray performs at the Billboard Music Awards.

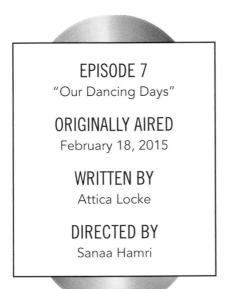

EPISODE 7
"Our Dancing Days"

ORIGINALLY AIRED
February 18, 2015

WRITTEN BY
Attica Locke

DIRECTED BY
Sanaa Hamri

As he prepares for an important showcase for potential investors, Lucious collapses, suffering from an illness brought on by the illegal ALS medication he is taking. Olivia abandons Lola at Empire Enterprises, and Lucious and Anika take the young girl in. Cookie tries to negotiate peace between Hakeem and Jamal before their big performance at the showcase, and attempts to keep an eye on Elle. Jamal, meanwhile, has his own crisis to deal with, as his boyfriend, upset that Jamal refuses to acknowledge their relationship publicly, moves out of their apartment. At the showcase, Anika sabotages Cookie's big moment by slipping drugs into Elle's drink, rendering her unable to perform. Just as he's about to give a big speech, Lucious loses his voice and asks Cookie to take his place. Rejecting the teleprompter, she gives an impassioned speech about the family roots and the future of Empire Enterprises. Later, Lucious opens up to his family about having ALS. The news causes Andre to freak out but brings Hakeem and Jamal together at last. After everyone leaves, Lucious and Cookie have a *heart-to-heart and rekindle the flame between them. Just as they're in the midst of getting it on, Anika comes home and finds the two in bed together.*

For all the familial affection that marks the last part of "Our Dancing Days," as Hakeem, Jamal, and Lucious share a tender moment between them, the Lyons are, more and more, revealing their truly selfish intentions. They're less concerned about the safety and health of their family members than they are with getting paid. Or as Cookie tells the two youngest sons, their squabbling during rehearsals for the big showcase is "coming between me and my money." Even as Rhonda tries to bring Andre back from his panic attack, her words of comfort—"You're going to run this company"—feel more like reassurance for herself than her husband. At least Lucious seems to be aware that he can't take his riches with him when he dies.

At the big investors showcase, though, none of that seems to matter. The idea is to dazzle all these moneyed venture capitalists and get them to crack open their checkbooks for Empire. Even the slightly critical song that Jamal and Hakeem perform, with its musical and lyrical references to Dire Straits's anti-commercialism hit "Money for Nothing," can't mask the real reason that everyone is there. Nor can Cookie's impassioned speech about her sons and her husband. Every moment of the presentation comes back to the main theme: Empire Enterprises is going to make all the assembled folks "filthy rich."

Nowhere is this self-centered attitude more apparent than with their treatment of Elle Dallas. Just one episode earlier, Cookie put her neck on the line to support an artist she claimed got her through her darkest hours in prison. It seemed like she really did want Elle to have a big comeback and reclaim some of the glory she had in her early days—but that was before Anika slipped some drugs into Elle's tea and strung her out. When that occurs, Cookie is more than willing to toss the singer aside, convinced she "shouldn't have trusted that junkie in the first place." It's telling, too, that this is the last we see or hear of Elle Dallas. She was only meaningful as long as she was both proving Cookie's worth to the company and potentially making them more money.

But a show like *Empire* isn't about empathy. This isn't a reflection of our lives or values; it's pure escapist entertainment in the mode of the numerous *Real Housewives* series or *Keeping Up with the Kardashians*. We watch these stories to see how the other half lives and (hopefully) see them make complete fools of themselves. As much as it sucks to watch Elle fall apart through no fault of her own, we are most likely ready to move on from her, as well.

What we are left with are the juiciest and most tawdry stories put forth yet. We have Jamal getting forced by his father to marry a woman as a way to hide his homosexuality, and potentially spawning a child as a result. We have Camilla potentially becoming a major character in the second half of the season, shaking things up even more between Hakeem and his parents. Most important, we have Cookie and Lucious hooking up—and Anika catching them in the act.

Jamal and Hakeem are, in so many ways, still a pair of spoiled rich kids. That even applies to Jamal during his independent phase, as he looks to stay away from his father's money (though driving off in that fancy SUV indicates that he's probably willing to get back into the fold). Their scandals in this episode only emphasize that. Hakeem thinks he can buy his way out of the doghouse with Camilla by offering up a specially cooked meal and a fancy necklace (one that in true narcissistic fashion spells out *Hakeem*). He has no clue how to negotiate an adult relationship. Not that Jamal does either. He only seems marginally upset by the fact that Michael is leaving him. You can almost sense some relief in his eyes as he watches his now-ex pack up.

What brings out Jamal's rich kid side, though, is him trying to figure out what to do with the little girl who has been dropped in his lap. For the most part, his dad's maid is handling things, but when his supposed daughter does get handed off to him, he can't get rid of her fast enough. "I have no idea what I'm doing," he says, passing the little lady off to Cookie. Poor guy has been coddled for so long, he has no sense of how to coddle someone else.

As for the sex scene that closes out the episode, everybody who was watching *Empire* from the beginning had to have seen that coming. Lucious has been flirtatious with his ex-wife ever since she got out of prison—at least when she's not kicking open the door of the conference room at Empire Enterprises and demanding his respect. How real is the connection between them, though? You might argue that Lucious is just trying to placate Cookie while fulfilling his narcissistic need to be wanted by every woman around. Seeing her openly flirt with Malcolm spurs him to turn things up a notch, not to mention all the emotions stirred up when he finally breaks the news of his illness to the family.

This relationship, such as it is, can't possibly last, though. The bad blood between Lucious and Cookie is still too potent, and he's too committed to moving forward with Anika. His fiancée, like the investors showcase, is a symbol of his success in completely escaping from the ghettos of Philadelphia, where Empire got its start. Life is too good for him in the skyscraper where the company has its offices and in the sprawling estate he calls home. Not even a taste of Cookie can make him forget that.

★ LUCIOUS LYON vs. HENRY II ★

As we mentioned earlier, *The Lion in Winter*, a play (and then a movie) about the twelfth-century king of England, was one of the inspirations behind the show—so the parallels between Henry and Lucious are a lot more obvious than many of the other empire builders we've talked about. Both men have children fighting to decide who among them will inherit the throne, both have enemies inside and outside the kingdom trying to undermine their rule, and both have fatal health issues (Henry was killed by a bleeding ulcer). If history proves anything, Lucious would do well to avoid handing control of Empire over to Hakeem, as it was Henry's youngest son, John, who ended up destroying his kingdom.

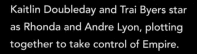

Kaitlin Doubleday and Trai Byers star as Rhonda and Andre Lyon, plotting together to take control of Empire.

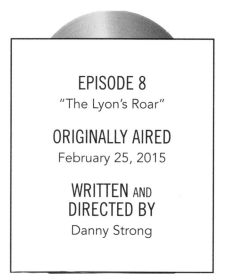

EPISODE 8
"The Lyon's Roar"

ORIGINALLY AIRED
February 25, 2015

WRITTEN AND DIRECTED BY
Danny Strong

*T*he morning after their dalliance, Cookie insists that if she and Lucious are going to continue a relationship, he needs to dump Anika. Andre and Vernon scheme to seize control of Empire Enterprises, with the idea of having the board of directors place the eldest Lyon son as interim CEO if something should happen to Lucious. Anika confronts Lucious about both sleeping with Cookie and having her father sign a key-man insurance policy. She insists that to make it to up to her, they must get married as soon as possible. Andre tries to secure the crucial final vote for his plan by offering up his wife to the husband of a board member, but Rhonda is revolted at the idea. Hakeem decides to show off his relationship with Camilla at the Empire white party, and Jamal finds a new love interest in Ryan, a filmmaker shooting a documentary about the Lyon legacy. Everything comes to a head at the party, with Cookie revealing to Anika that she slept with Lucious a second time, Cookie dressing down Camilla, and Jamal coming out of the closet onstage using a rewritten version of one of his father's songs. The next day, Lucious tells Andre that he's never going to be CEO. If that weren't *enough, Anika finishes off the episode by making the ultimate betrayal: visiting Billy Beretti's apartment.*

If there is a crucial episode of the first season, where all the storylines from the previous weeks finally come together, it is "The Lyon's Roar." All the drama of the past seven weeks comes to a peak; everything that happens next, right up to the season finale, is fallout from this hour.

The most significant moment, not only for the show but for television in general, is Jamal publicly coming out. Yes, there have been gay characters on network series before *Empire*, but Jamal coming out directly addresses the stigma that gay people face in the hip-hop and R&B worlds. Even with artists like Mykki Blanco and Big Freedia capturing mainstream attention, homophobia is still there. As gay rapper Cakes Da Killa told VH1, "It is definitely still there. I just think now . . . it's not as blatant."

Of course, the prejudice often doesn't extend to lesbians or bisexual women, at least not as intensely. It says everything that when Lucious finds out that Tiana is bi, he doesn't freak out but instead encourages Hakeem to get in on the action—then starts thinking about how he can market it. The day after Jamal comes out, on the other hand, finds Lucious skulking into the office like he had just been caught having a drunken freak-out by TMZ. That's why Jamal's public declaration, as well as the one Jussie Smollett made on *The Ellen DeGeneres Show* some weeks later are so important. If the tide is going to shift on this issue, people need to be more open about it.

Lucious's mournful reaction to Jamal's coming out is unsurprising—the show has firmly established by now that, as far as Lucious is concerned, everything going on in the world only matters insofar as it affects him personally. Or as Hakeem puts it,

"All Dad cares about is making music and money." And as Jamal warns his mother, after finding out that she and Lucious have been sleeping together, "That man is incapable of loving anyone but himself." Just watch when Lucious gets called out by Anika about his hookup with Cookie. He reels and blubbers, acts oh-so-sorry for what he has done, and promises, of course, that he's never going to do it again. Twenty minutes later, he has pinned Cookie up against the soundboard in the studio. It's actually kind of impressive how much Lucious is able to get away with and still be forgiven by the women in his life. That's either hard-core forgiveness on their part or sheer delusion.

Of course, by the end, Lucious doesn't have either woman. He already blew off Cookie, and Anika decides to exact some revenge by ditching Lucious for Beretti. Stir in his shame at having his son announce to the world that he's gay and the discovery that another of his sons has been scheming behind his back to take over control of the company, and you almost start to feel sorry for the guy—until you remember how awful he has been to everyone around him, except for Lola, his alleged granddaughter. He doesn't care who he hurts until it starts to have a negative effect on *his* life. If ever there was a fictional character in need of a little just punishment, it's Lucious Lyon. By the end of the episode, close to burning his last bridge with Cookie, he even turns his nose up at celebrating the one thing that makes his company special—the Lyon family dynamic. Anika might not need to hook up with Beretti as a way to bring down Empire and her ex. At this rate, Lucious could easily do it on his own.

Meanwhile, Andre is the character you should be empathizing with. There's something actually relatable in the fate of a guy who has to sit back and watch his father and brothers get all the glory thanks to their musical talent. Even with all of his hard work making sure the bills are getting paid and the important decisions are getting made, Andre still hasn't managed to earn the respect and support of his father. His unstable emotional state just makes him more pitiable.

Then again, this is a guy who's willing to pimp his wife out to get ahead and who then acts surprised when she decides she doesn't want to play those games anymore. And he's the guy who likes to sit in the recording studio, lamenting his lot in life while playing Russian roulette with a .45.

Danny Strong, the writer and director of this episode, deserves credit for finding little moments of peace and happiness amid all the clamor and bombast and sniping. The scene between Jamal and Lola is very, very sweet. And there is definitely something cool when Jamal, Hakeem, and their parents have a small bonding moment as they sing the chorus to one of Lucious's songs in the studio. If there's one element that often seems overlooked in this very dramatic show, it is those little moments of quiet, when no one has an agenda or is trying to game someone else by playing nice. It proves at least that inside all the scenery chewing, acting, and slick music video–like performance sequences, Strong and cocreator Lee Daniels still thread a small sliver of hope into the hardened, often cynical heart that *Empire* usually exhibits.

GUEST STAR

M. Emmet Walsh

If this veteran character actor looks familiar to you, don't be surprised. Since kicking off his career in the late '60s, Walsh has played roles both big and small in more than two hundred films and TV series. Some of his more high-profile work has been as the apothecary in Baz Luhrmann's fast-paced modern-day adaptation of *Romeo + Juliet*, the madman who tries to gun down Navin Johnson (Steve Martin) after picking his name out of the phone book in *The Jerk*, and the sleazy private detective in the early Coen Brothers classic *Blood Simple*.

Jussie Smollett performs with Estelle at the Billboard Music Awards.

EPISODE 9
"Unto the Breach"

ORIGINALLY AIRED
March 4, 2015

WRITTEN BY
David Rambo

DIRECTED BY
Anthony Hemingway

*A*ll seems well in Lucious's home, with wedding plans under way, until Cookie bursts in to tell him that Anika has been colluding with Beretti. This sends Empire Enterprises into crisis mode, trying to find new artists and save the ones they have before Creedmoor poaches them. Andre, meanwhile, decides he's had enough of the meds for his bipolar disorder and flushes them down the toilet. Everyone else hits the streets: Cookie stops by a recording studio to try to win back an artist who's on the fence, while Jamal uses his boyfriend to get an audience with a British soul singer named Delphine. Hakeem brings Travie Wild to the office, and while he initially agrees to join Empire, he is soon being flown out of the country by Beretti. Back at the offices, the three Lyon brothers get stuck in an elevator, which pushes an already manic Andre over the edge. Once freed, the security detail has to keep him in check until an ambulance can come and escort him to a psychiatric ward. Empire scores some major wins in the midst of all this, as Cookie and Hakeem convince Tiana to stick with the label and Lucious helps win over Delphine.

Considering all the drama and all the intense moments of the previous week, it would make sense to have Lucious and his family quietly reassessing things and picking up the pieces after the eventful white party. Instead, we get one small respite, with a giddy Lucious and Anika talking wedding plans before—*boom*—Cookie kicks her way in and sets this bullet train of an episode in motion.

The whole thing plays like a heist film, or like the last episode of *Mad Men's* third season when Don Draper, Roger Sterling, and the rest of the gang decide to start a new advertising firm and spend much of the hour gathering materials and scrambling to retain their clients. "Unto the Breach" is edgier than that, although it's not hard to imagine Don spending an afternoon trading shots of purple drank with a bunch of rappers if it meant holding on to a hot commodity.

Another way Lucious is like the men of Sterling Cooper (maybe most men, really) is his belief he can get away with everything, followed by the freak-out when someone close to him acts just as ruthlessly. We get an unfiltered glimpse of it when Lucious practically goes down on his knees, begging Anika to rethink her plans to leave him and his company in the lurch. It's a moment that says everything you really need to know about the Empire CEO. He's not concerned about losing his ladylove or seeking forgiveness for his misdeeds. Even with his weepy worry that she could expose the fraud her father committed, all he wants to do is make sure he isn't going to lose any money because of her.

After that, the old vendetta with Beretti kicks in and it becomes an all-out war, with Empire's only goal being to make more money than their closest competitor. Think about that for a minute: they actually have a PowerPoint slide up on the screen showing the net worth of each company—and freak out because they are a few million behind Creedmoor. It's a reflection on how a lot of the labels in the hip-hop world define themselves strictly by how much money they can claim to have in their bank accounts (the few record labels still around, that is). And it's what makes the perspective of Travie Wild, a rock star Empire is trying to sign, that's thrown into the mix of this episode so interesting.

As Travie points out, he doesn't need an actual label anymore, let alone one that would claim 30 percent of his profits. The Internet has completely leveled the playing field for musicians, putting the power back into their hands. A venture like Empire Enterprises, even with its promise of a 360 deal that allows the label and artist to split the profits from every revenue stream available (album sales, downloads, streaming, concert tickets, merchandise, etc.), is still working from an outdated business model. And yet, even after making that case so strongly, Travie turns around and goes with Creedmoor, undoubtedly at just about the same terms Empire is prepared to give him.

Still, it is surprisingly great to see Empire score the big wins that they do. The scenes with Cookie and the rapper getting drunk together are absolutely hilarious and so is watching Hakeem run interference with Anika while Cookie works her magic with Tiana. Hakeem even has a chance to humble himself before his ex-girlfriend, proving that behind that thuggish demeanor lies a surprisingly tender heart. Even better, though, is the scene where Lucious and Jamal sit down at Leviticus with the soul singer Delphine, a meeting that turns into a spirited sing-along to what has become the show's signature song, "You're So Beautiful." Who wouldn't get swept up in a moment like that, as all of Lucious's empty talk about the power of music actually comes to life, if only for a few minutes?

Writer David Rambo and director Anthony Hemingway quickly bring the episode back down to Earth with the next scene, with a tour de force performance by Trai Byers as Andre going completely off the rails, tossing papers and basketballs around, ranting and raving. The quick shift from the glitz of the nightclub where Lucious, Delphine, and Jamal sing joyously to Andre losing all sense of himself in the boardroom is perfectly jarring—and a little terrifying, once he gets in Lucious's face and threatens to reveal the secret about Bunkie's murder.

Impressively, much of the scene was improvised. "Rambo's script gave the actors an amazing launch pad," Byers told the *Hollywood Reporter*, "but we had to fuel it. We had to put a little extra something there to ultimately get where we needed to go and touch people and make this an unforgettable moment in television." It certainly is a scene that is hard to shake, which is saying something for a show that had already served up dozens of indelible scenes over the course of its first season.

★ LUCIOUS LYON VS. HENRY V ★

Where Lucious feels he is entitled to dominion over the world of hip-hop, during his nine-year reign as king of England, Henry V felt that his claim to occupy France was a legitimate one. This comparison might be a bit of a stretch; after all, Lucious's battle with Creedmoor hasn't erupted into a bloody war (although there was that drive-by). Still, both men are excellent case studies in how men in power can begin to feel that the rest of the world should simply bend to their will—and when it doesn't, that can start all manner of ugly conflicts.

GUEST STAR

Estelle

Thought she has been making music in her native UK since 2000, Estelle didn't break through in the US until almost a decade later, when she scored a Top 10 (and Grammy-winning) hit with "American Boy," her collaboration with Kanye West. Since that breakthrough, she's been an in-demand guest vocalist, working with everyone from hip-hop icons Gucci Mane and Busta Rhymes to EDM superstar David Guetta. These days she's balancing her work as a musician with her budding acting career. In addition to her appearance on *Empire* as Delphine, Estelle is the voice of Garnet on the Cartoon Network series *Steven Universe*.

"Cookie is bold and crazy, and she loves the struggle," Taraji P. Henson told *W* magazine. "She started from nothing, and now she's at the top. In that way, we're alike: Cookie is the American Dream."

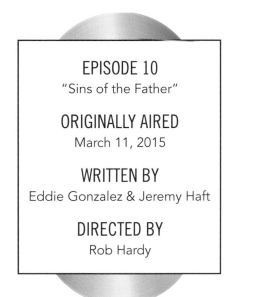

EPISODE 10
"Sins of the Father"

ORIGINALLY AIRED
March 11, 2015

WRITTEN BY
Eddie Gonzalez & Jeremy Haft

DIRECTED BY
Rob Hardy

On the eve of Empire Enterprises going public, the Lyon family tries to convince Andre to join them in signing the paperwork, but he refuses to leave the psychiatric hospital, giving proxy for his shares over to Rhonda. Lucious, meanwhile, decides that he's going to ask Cookie to remarry him so they can raise Lola together. Jamal has similar plans for Lola, wanting to take responsibility and raise her on his own. Malcolm finally reveals his feelings for Cookie. Olivia tries to leave the city but is caught by her abusive ex, Reg, who insists they go find Lola. The two track down Vernon at a bar and convince him to take them to Lucious's home. With the family gathering at Lucious's house, all hell breaks loose. Hakeem arrives with Camilla and a new song that they've been working on together. Lucious smells something fishy and tries to pay Camilla to go away. She does leave, but not before tearing up the check. Rhonda then figures out that Lucious took shares away from all three of the boys. Finally, Vernon brings Olivia and Reg to the house, causing a standoff that compels Lucious to admit Lola is actually his daughter.

Of all the awful and sometimes terrifying things that Lucious says, the worst is when he tells Camilla, "I'm making Hakeem in my image." Can you think of anything more awful for his son? Here, after all, is a guy who is more than happy to take every bit of the credit for Empire's success, but who refuses to even admit that his oldest son has a serious mental disorder, who blanches at the idea of Jamal raising a little girl because of his gay "lifestyle," and who refuses to acknowledge that Lola is actually his own daughter until someone starts waving a gun around. Making that comment to Camilla, furthermore, he completely dismisses the notion that she and Hakeem might have real feelings for each other and is more than happy to dole out a healthy chunk of money to make her disappear.

As far as role models go, there are few worse than Lucious Lyon.

Unfortunately, everyone at Empire Enterprises has to go through him if they want to make lots of money with this IPO—and they don't even manage to make that happen. The whole episode has a dreamlike logic to it; every time they get close to signing the papers, something comes up or someone appears to interrupt them. If they were faithful people, they might think that God is giving them a sign.

Or you could say karma is coming around to finally kick Lucious in the ass. He's a bad, bad man who gets away with murder and justifies it to himself by claiming he's just trying to do what's best for the family and for the company. What makes it possibly worse is that strange tearful choke that Terrence Howard gets in his voice whenever a scene calls for him to be intense or emotional.

The thing that does Lucious in every time is his need for absolute control over every aspect of the lives of the people around him—and stupidly thinking they'll just go along with it. Notice that he's actually surprised when Camilla tears up the check he handed her and throws it in his face? Or his pained expression when Rhonda calls him out for taking away stock from his sons to give to his ex-wife? He even manages to look confused when Cookie isn't overjoyed to learn that he's making her head of A&R and that he wants to remarry her. Instinctually, she can tell Lucious isn't *really* doing it because he "doesn't want to lose her again." Once a player, always a player.

"Sins of the Father" is also an excellent example of how well the writers for *Empire* handle all the female characters on the show. Other than Cookie, not all of the women who come in and out of the lives of the Lyon men are necessarily looking to siphon money away from this incredibly rich family. Olivia doesn't bring Lola into their lives looking for a handout; she just wants to protect her little girl from a dangerous situation. Camilla may have some strange ideas about where Hakeem should take his career, but they come from a place of genuine affection and appreciation for his talents. Even Rhonda seems to have a change of heart about her power-hungry ways with the realization of just how much of herself she is giving away when she throws herself at other men and women for the sake of conquering Empire.

A similar self-realization explains why Andre wants to stay in the hospital rather than deal with any of the IPO business. For the first time, he is surrounded by people who simply want him to get better. After years of dealing with folks who only had money and power on their minds, this has to be a welcome shock to the system. Michelle White, the music therapist, played by guest star Jennifer Hudson, offers a powerful symbol for this new environment. When she locks the door and comes in very, very close to Andre, he—like just about everybody watching at home—is sure they are about to tear each other's clothes off.

Instead, she only wants to pray—and where once he might have reacted angrily to having been "led on" by her, Andre's ready to embrace a new way of living.

His brother Jamal shows signs of a similarly flexible spirit. As he realizes that being open about his sexuality hasn't caused the walls of his world to come crumbling down, he can take on an even bigger life change in trying to take care of Lola on his own. The scenes with Jamal and Lola, especially when he and Hakeem work together to sing her to sleep, are perfect moments of levity and joy, moments this episode needs, with all the darkness permeating the rest of the hour. It's too bad that Lucious's coming forward and admitting he's Lola's real father might mean fewer scenes between her and Jamal in the future.

After everything that goes down in this episode, it's a wonder anyone would want to be a part of Empire Enterprises, let alone pitch themselves as the right person to lead it once Lucious cannot. They're getting to see firsthand just how much greed corrupts people, how millions of dollars can somehow convince a person that every decision they make is the right one—or, if it turns out to be a mistake, they can always buy their way out of it. And, as we're seeing in Lucious's panicked eyes when guns are being waved around and he's not getting his way, the guilt accumulated in a life lived that way is far too much for anyone to bear.

GUEST STAR

Mary J. Blige

Although she has only a small role in this episode, singing alongside Lucious during a flashback that spells out his relationship with Olivia, Mary J. Blige is instantly recognizable. That's because, since 1989, she's been one of the most successful soul/R&B singers in the world. Eight of her studio albums have gone platinum, and every one of her LPs lands near the top of the *Billboard* charts. Blige is also versatile enough to be able to work with hard-core rappers like Method Man and 50 Cent, rockers U2, and EDM duo Disclosure. She's also a fixture on the big and small screen, including in a key supporting role in Tyler

Perry's *I Can Do Bad All by Myself* and as the wife of Malcolm X in the Lifetime TV movie *Betty and Coretta*.

GUEST STAR

Jennifer Hudson

This Chicago native's first blushes with fame arrived when she appeared on the third season of *American Idol*. Though she finished in seventh place, she's arguably gone on to have a far more successful post-*Idol* career than any of her competitors, with three top 10 albums, an invitation to sing the national anthem at Super Bowl XLII, and a star on the Hollywood Walk of Fame. Hudson has also thrived as an actor, winning the Academy Award for her performance as Effie White in the film adaptation of *Dreamgirls* and playing opposite her future *Empire* costar Terrence Howard in the 2011 film *Winnie Mandela*.

★ LUCIOUS LYON VS. MARK ANTONY ★

In this episode, Camilla compares her relationship with Hakeem to that of Cleopatra and Mark Antony's—which, as Jamal observes, doesn't bode well for either of them. Antony isn't all that much like Lucious; he was far more loyal to his former commander, Julius Caesar, than Lucious would ever be to Billy Beretti. But, like most emperors, Lucious and Antony do share a tendency to discard the women in their lives when they've worn out their welcome—or when a more alluring option presents itself.

"I think people get Cookie," Taraji P. Henson said in an interview with *Time*. "She's not a malicious person. She's just real. She shoots straight from the hip, and . . . nine times out of ten she's right!"

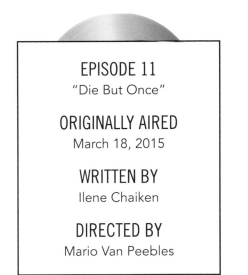

EPISODE 11
"Die But Once"

ORIGINALLY AIRED
March 18, 2015

WRITTEN BY
Ilene Chaiken

DIRECTED BY
Mario Van Peebles

*L*ucious finds himself stuck trying to write a song for his big tribute concert, while Cookie is off on a romantic weekend with Malcolm. While Hakeem prepares to release his debut album, Jamal gets his own record out and begins promoting it. Beretti files an injunction blocking Lucious from performing any songs he recorded with Creedmoor at the show. Then Hakeem, freestyling onstage, calls out his father, and Lucious responds by punching his son in the face—prompting him to defect from Empire and sign with Beretti. In his desperation to find Cookie, Lucious learns she was with Malcolm and loses it, firing her and kicking her out. Later, Lucious and Jamal help each other find inspiration, for both music and the future of Empire Enterprises. That leads the younger Lyon to confront Beretti and threaten to throw him off a balcony unless he signs over Lucious's master recordings to Empire. At that same time, Lucious searches for Hakeem and finds his son in bed with Anika. If that weren't enough, Lucious also learns he was misdiagnosed and doesn't have ALS. The treatment for his real ailment, though, puts him in a drug-induced haze where he confesses to Bunkie's murder. Overhearing this, Cookie prepares to smother Lucious with a pillow.

With the flurry of activity and information and gasp-inducing moments thrown into "Die But Once," it's as if the producers anticipated that by this point they would have reached their highest audience numbers yet and wanted to throw as much at them as they could. In the best way possible, it has the effect of sensory overload, stuffing us full of incident and drama and still leaving us begging for more.

The key to "Die But Once" is Lucious's hubris. Over the course of the episode, he says he's going to be a god, the messiah, bigger than Jesus, a phoenix rising from the ashes—and scoffs at the thought that Andre would want to seek out something to worship other than his father. Lucious thinks so much of himself that he expects his ex-wife to drop everything she's doing and rush to his side just because he's stuck on a song, which makes him sound more like a petulant child than any kind of deity. Is it any wonder, then, that almost everyone in the show is looking forward to his death? Little do they know that he's going to be sticking around a while longer, now that he knows he has a much more treatable condition. Of course, when Lucious gets the news, he's not grateful or excited for a new lease on life. Instead, he gets mad at the doctor for making a mistake, then starts laughing maniacally. Now is his chance to tighten his grasp on Empire.

The most difficult thing to witness is how the apple didn't fall far from the tree with his two youngest sons. You might expect it from Hakeem, considering how raw he has been throughout, and how angry he was at both his father and Camilla for the deal they made (though he doesn't know that she didn't take the money). Given all that, signing with Creedmoor seems like the appropriate "fuck you" to Lucious, as does seducing Anika. Both these actions are power moves, attempts to prove himself as an individual outside of Empire, out from under his father's shadow. But Jamal's transition into a cold-blooded "monster"

(Lucious's word) is genuinely shocking. The moment when he and his father work on a song together becomes a kind of transfer of energy, a way for the elder Lyon to push the younger into acts you couldn't imagine the man who sang Lola to sleep so sweetly in the previous episode committing. Yet there he is, ready to throw Beretti off a balcony and making his own sexual power move against Lucious by having sex with Ryan on his father's desk.

In *Empire*, it's not just power that corrupts, it's Lucious. He can't leave anyone alone, and needs to drag them all down to his craven level. You can hear it in the oily, seductive tone he uses around Cookie's sister, or in his efforts to woo Andre back to Empire because he doesn't want anyone worshipping another god above him. He hits his son where it hurts most, appealing to our basest, fame-hungry instincts by offering the music therapist who brought Andre back from the brink a contract.

What makes all of this weigh even heavier is that there are no real moments of sweetness or light to counter the darkness. The attempts to add a bit of sexiness with Cookie and Malcolm's hookup, or the stray bits of comedy from Becky and Porsha, don't land—by now viewers have gotten used to the idea that something bad will happen to these folks no matter what, that every moment of joy will be followed by the rug getting pulled out from under their feet.

The other dramatic moments in this episode are almost laughably handled. The ALS misdiagnosis, for example, feels like it comes out of nowhere, and Lucious's drug-induced confession is as silly as it gets, with Bunkie appearing at the foot of Lucious's bed, a spotlight trained on him. You might get away with that sort of thing in the Shakespearean-style dramas *Empire* draws some of its inspiration from, but it really doesn't work on television.

The cliffhanger at the end doesn't hold water, either. As good as it might feel to see Lucious go out in such an inglorious fashion, there's no way anyone can seriously believe he'll be dead in the next episode. Jamal and Hakeem might have begun to show some aspects of their father's personality in their own behavior, but they're no substitute for the real thing. *Empire* just isn't *Empire* without Lucious and his oily, villainous presence for everyone else in the show to bounce off, work against, and trade barbs with. Die? More likely, Lucious will come back stronger than ever, ready to mow down anyone foolish enough to get in his way.

GUEST STAR

Snoop Dogg

One of the most recognizable faces and names in hip-hop, Snoop Dogg became an instant icon after his appearances on Dr. Dre's 1992 classic *The Chronic*. In the years since, Snoop has been a fixture on stage and screen, releasing thirteen albums, producing three TV series (including the reality show *Snoop Dogg's Father Hood*), and appearing in films such as *Half Baked*, *Training Day*, and *Starsky & Hutch*.

GUEST STAR

Mario Van Peebles

The director of this episode, Mario Van Peebles, has logged plenty of time in front of and behind the camera. As an actor, he has scored notable roles in films like Clint Eastwood's *Heartbreak Ridge*, *Highlander: The Final Dimension*, and the Will Smith–starring biopic *Ali*, as well as on TV in *All My Children*, *Damages*, and *Nashville*. No stranger to small-screen directing,

Van Peebles has also helmed a number of feature films, such as cult classics *New Jack City* and *All Things Fall Apart*, the drama starring rapper 50 Cent.

★ LUCIOUS LYON vs. CAESAR ★

When Julius Caesar took on the position of dictator, it was only supposed to be a temporary role. Instead, he gave himself the job for life. As much as Lucious talks about his willingness to pass Empire Enterprises on to one of his sons, his actions throughout the first season of *Empire* indicate they're probably going to have to pry his cold, dead hands off the CEO's desk. Lucious has avoided shuffling off this mortal coil due to ALS, gun threats, and an attempt on his life by Cookie. So unless, like Caesar, a bunch of his advisers and friends join forces to take him down, he's probably going to be in charge for a long, long time.

Waiting for production on the second season to begin, *Empire* co-stars Terrence Howard and Taraji P. Henson kept in the media spotlight, co-hosting Spike TV's Guys Choice Awards.

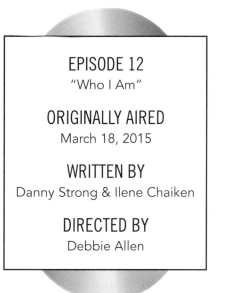

EPISODE 12
"Who I Am"

ORIGINALLY AIRED
March 18, 2015

WRITTEN BY
Danny Strong & Ilene Chaiken

DIRECTED BY
Debbie Allen

With a new lease on life, Lucious attempts to reconcile with his sons. He apologies to Hakeem for holding him back and for getting rid of Camilla, then gives him a private jet. He apologizes to Andre for trying to tear apart his faith in God and sets up the Lyon Foundation for his eldest son to control. And he names Jamal as his successor as CEO. The next day at Empire Enterprises' offices, Jamal does his best to calm Andre and Hakeem, who are both mad he's been put in charge. Lucious then shares the security footage of Cookie trying to kill him, and has her thrown out of the building. Immediately, the FBI pick her up and try to convince her to snitch on her ex-husband for Bunkie's murder. Rhonda decides to leave Andre, upset that he let Empire go without a fight. Cookie, Anika, Andre, and Hakeem join forces to try to set up a hostile takeover of Empire. Vernon visits Andre in an attempt to get him to accept Jamal being in charge, and the two end up fighting. Rhonda shows up and, trying to protect her husband, ends up killing Vernon. Andre is about to call the cops, but she talks him out of it, and announces that she's pregnant. Finally, at the tribute show celebrating his career, Lucious is arrested backstage for Bunkie's murder.

How do you wrap up the first season of a show already overstuffed with drama, intrigue, murder, social commentary, instantly quotable dialogue, and hot R&B, soul, and hip-hop tunes? You give viewers more of the same—a lot more. The *Empire* season finale plays out almost as if the producers knew they would have their biggest audience yet and decided to pull out all the stops for them. The only cliffhanger that really matters, though, is Lucious's arrest on suspicion of murder—and, of course, it's going to be harder to prove he did it now that Vernon, their star witness, has vanished.

Sure, there's that potential hostile takeover of Empire, headed up by the surprising alliance between Cookie, Andre, Hakeem, and Anika. But that's far less interesting than finding out how Lucious will get out of his bind and what kind of hell he'll rain down upon his duplicitous family members once he's released.

With the benefit of hindsight, we can see how Lee Daniels, Danny Strong, and the rest of the show's writing team were setting up the way the allegiances would shake out at the end of the season. It's almost as if they'd been taking notes straight from the Aaron Spelling playbook. As the story unfolds over these twelve episodes, it makes sense that Jamal and Lucious would be simpatico even after all the friction and all the bile they have spewed at each other, and that the two younger Lyon brothers, who were so supportive of each other for so long, would now be at odds.

The only development that does come as a small surprise is when Cookie and Anika decide to work together to take down Lucious—but not before their long-simmering tensions boil over into a hair-pulling, pearl-necklace-destroying scrap. Another move straight out of *Dynasty*, recalling the classic brawls between Krystle and Alexis, and as satisfying as it is hilarious.

For all the fireworks in this episode, the most powerful moment in it is also the quietest one. Right before Lucious gets taken away by the police, he has a heart-to-heart with Jamal, expressing regret for how he has treated his son. "It's hard enough growing up a black man in this world," he offers, "but to be a homosexual on top of it . . ." Hardly justification for some of the rotten things he's done and said to Jamal, but at least he's trying. It's a long way from that moment in the first episode when Lucious shoved his son into the trash can. In an interview with the *Philadelphia Inquirer*, Lee Daniels talked about how he wished his own father were alive to see the show, knowing that they might be able to finally put their past disagreements to rest. In fiction, sometimes, we can imagine the moments of reconciliation we don't achieve in real life. (Although, it's simplistic to say he created a happy ending for himself—not least of all because it's Danny Strong and Ilene Chaiken who are credited with writing this episode.)

"Who I Am" also gives Jamal a moment of pure triumph. As if his success as a recording artist and his ascension to the role of CEO at Empire isn't enough, he gets to show up a homophobic rapper who dropped out of the Lucious Lyon tribute concert because he didn't want to be associated with a "batty man" (the Jamaican patois term for a gay or effeminate male). The scene where he battles the rapper onstage gives viewers a small victory in the midst of all the dark revelations, accidental killings, and angry verbal sparring going on around it.

It's a scene that fits neatly into Jamal's character trajectory. Out of all the characters in the show, he is the only one who has truly evolved and, for want of a better term, grown up, by the end of this first season. Now that his reluctance to be out about his sexuality is behind him, he has a chance to really put his musical stamp on Empire Enterprises. As the show comes to its final montage, you can see the confidence with which he takes control of an A&R meeting.

Despite everything that has happened to them, the rest of the main characters are pretty much exactly where they were at the beginning—with one significant reversal of fortune. Lucious is still a dangerous, angry man, but now he's the one behind bars, while catty, sexy Cookie has settled into her ex-husband's gigantic mansion.

GUEST STAR

Juicy J

Juicy J and the rest of Three 6 Mafia nabbed a Best Original Song award for "It's Hard out Here for a Pimp," written for *Hustle & Flow*. As great as that accolade was, the Tennessee-based rapper and producer will be better remembered as one of the architects of the current sound of hip-hop, crafting beats for the likes of Ludacris, Odd Future member Hodgy Beats, Lil Wayne, Wale, and Nicki Minaj.

GUEST STAR

Patti LaBelle

The High Priestess of Good Vibrations, Patti LaBelle has done it all in her lengthy musical career. Her group LaBelle was the first African American group to be featured on the cover of *Rolling Stone*, thanks to their sci-fi-inspired flair and iconic hits like "Lady Marmalade." Her solo career has been a sensation as well, with massive hits like "New Attitude" and her duet with Michael McDonald, "On My Own." As an actress, LaBelle played a key supporting role in the film *A Soldier's Story* and has been seen more recently on *American Horror Story: Freak Show* and as a competitor on *Dancing with the Stars*.

THE MUSIC

When the news broke in early 2014 that Timbaland would be over-seeing the music for a new television drama that aimed to be the "hip-hop *Dynasty*," you could almost hear the collective sigh of relief among music fans. It's easy to do hip-hop badly, especially nowadays when every laptop comes preloaded with easy-to-use software like GarageBand that lets anyone with a fleeting interest in making a beat or writing a rhyme knock out a track in a half hour. But Timbaland (born Timothy Mosley) is the real deal. As a rapper, producer, and songwriter, he's been a constant presence on the radio since the mid-'90s, when he started making chart-topping singles with artists like Aaliyah, Ginuwine, and his most frequent collaborator, Missy Elliott. Over the years, he has anointed dozens of kings and queens in the worlds of hip-hop and pop—he helped turn Justin Timberlake into a megawatt superstar, brought Nelly Furtado to the dance clubs of the world, and has added his sleek buzzing and clicking beats to tracks by everyone from Madonna and Björk to Coldplay and Soundgarden frontman Chris Cornell.

He was the perfect choice to bring musical legitimacy to a prime-time soap opera about a hip-hop record label and its stable of hit-making artists—yet *Empire*'s cocreator Lee Daniels had no idea who he was. (As he told *Entertainment Weekly*, "I'm stuck in the world of Diana Ross and Donna Summer.") It was Daniels's children who convinced him to hire Timbaland, a decision that paid instant dividends, when the producer brought in his first finished tracks just three days after he'd been hired.

That kind of work ethic proved critical in the months ahead, as each episode of *Empire* required lots of musical material. The pilot alone features a dozen original songs. That's where someone with Timbaland's extensive contacts comes in very handy. To help churn out the tunes, he called on friends like longtime collaborator Jim Beanz, R&B artist Raphael Saadiq, Tricky Stewart (the man behind Beyoncé's "Single Ladies (Put a Ring on It)"), and singer-songwriter Claude Kelly. While he let this all-star lineup run free, Timbaland had a hand in every song that made it on the air. "I oversee it," he told *Vanity Fair*. "I listen to it, I change a word here, or add something to the beat, switch that over there."

Sometimes Daniels and his team could only give Timbaland and his people a rough guideline of the themes or plot of each episode, and they would be forced to write the songs from those hints. "It takes a while to write a song according to the story notes or emotions that the song needs to help accomplish," Fox's senior VP of TV music told *Variety*. "We have to have those songs ready to go before anyone can step in front of a camera." It gave them plenty of leeway, but both the lyricists and the screenwriters had to tweak their material to make sure everything matched up in the final version.

The music team also needed to consider that their songs would be used to advance the show's story line or enable characters like Jamal and Hakeem to express emotions they wouldn't otherwise be able to talk aloud. The most obvious instance of this is when Jamal finally comes out of the closet at an Empire Enterprises party by singing one of his father's songs, "You're So Beautiful," rewriting a key lyric to say, "It's the kind of song that makes a man love a man." It's a perfect dramatic moment, as Jamal not only finds the courage to stand up to Lucious, but he does it with a song that's already been established within the show as a hit for his father.

Jamal has many such musically dramatic moments throughout the series. He turns his nose up at his father's riches in the song "Keep Your Money" and lays out his frustrations about Lucious's dismissal of his homosexuality with "Good Enough." At the end of the season, when he takes control of Empire Enterprises with his father's blessing, the defiant and powerful "Nothing to Lose" stokes his internal fires.

Hakeem, on the other hand, is a lot more in-your-face than his older brother, willing to call Cookie and everyone else out for their sins and missteps. His songs tend to give him space to brag about his wealth and sexual prowess (at least as much as network standards allow), but he does get a couple of chances to musically vent. After he finds out that his girlfriend, Tiana, is having a relationship with another woman, for example, he hits the studio and spews out "Can't Truss 'Em," a vicious attack on the ladies in his life. Later, when Empire presents itself to potential investors, Hakeem and Jamal provide a little sly commentary about the proceedings with a rewrite of Dire Straits's anticommercialist pop anthem "Money for Nothing."

Empire fans didn't just content themselves with listening to the music while watching the show, either. Fox wisely took the same approach they had with a previous hit series, *Glee*, placing the key songs from each episode for sale on iTunes the same night it aired, and making sure the entire soundtrack album was available not long after the season finale's last cut to black. It shot right to #1 on the *Billboard* charts and turned *Empire's* young cast—particularly Jussie Smollett—into real-world pop stars.

Of course, on the show, everything the Lyons put their hands or voices on turns out to be a hit; every song gets the party jumping or has the club clamoring for more. And we all know the real world doesn't work that way. Even someone like Madonna doesn't hit the bull's-eye every time; in fact, the success of the *Empire* soundtrack kept her own new album, *Rebel Heart*, from the top of the *Billboard* album charts.

For all the soundtrack's commercial success, though, critical acclaim has been tougher to come by. Some reviewers, like Craig Jenkins at Pitchfork and Kyle Anderson at *Entertainment Weekly*, have praised the show's music and its "stirring hip-hop soul revivals." But most appraisals have been mixed, with David Turner at the deadspin.com column "The Concourse" registering a typical complaint. "No Apologies," a duet between Hakeem and Jamal, "sounds five years out of date," Turner wrote. "Too many of these allegedly modern hits . . . come off like leftovers from [Justin Timberlake's] *The 20/20 Experience* or Rihanna's *Good Girl Gone Bad*," albums that came out in 2013 and 2007, respectively.

He might have a point. Some of the show's tunes can sound overheated or undercooked, and the production has largely bypassed new trends in hip-hop like the emergence of trap music or the noisier tracks that Kanye and groups like Death Grips are creating. But that's probably exactly the approach to take, really. Timbaland and his team could count on *Empire* pulling in a huge audience from African American communities on the East and West Coasts, along with big cities like Atlanta and Chicago—those parts of the country that have vibrant hip-hop scenes where cutting-edge sounds flourish.

But *Empire* was looking for more than just that audience, aiming to bring in the folks from everywhere else, people who only pay attention to top 40 hip-hop sounds that might be a little behind the curve artistically but, more important, are still mass-market friendly. Timbaland and the entire crew of *Empire* seemed to know that if they could get those viewers tuning in week to week, and buying mp3s of their favorite songs the same night, they would have a serious hit on their hands. Sure enough, *Empire* took off like a rocket, Jussie Smollett is well on his way to becoming a household name, and kids across the country know the chorus of "Drip Drop."

Empire musical director Timbaland

THE FUTURE

After *Empire*'s triumphant first season, the show's fans have been eager to find out what's coming next for the Lyon family. Does Jamal stand a chance fighting off the hostile takeover whipped up by Cookie, Anika, and his brothers? What impact will running the day-to-day operations of Empire Enterprises have on his music career? Will Andre and Rhonda continue to hide their accidental killing of Vernon? Will Lucious remain in prison, or will he find a way out?

The show's creators have remained tight-lipped about the specifics of the plotlines they've been cooking up for season two. Instead, when they've spoken to the media, they've emphasized that their goal is to simply maintain the mood and quality they achieved during the first season. As cocreator Danny Strong put it when discussing the show at the ATX Television Festival in Austin, Texas, at the start of the summer, they knew not to attempt to make it bigger and better—all that would do is "make it worse and lamer." But from the few details that have come out in the months after the season finale, it looks like *Empire* will expand in several small but substantive ways.

It's going to be a longer season—eighteen episodes this time around, instead of twelve—and it will be split into two parts, with a midseason cliffhanger separating the arcs.

The show's musical team will get a boost with the addition of R&B artist Ne-Yo, and Danny Strong has said that he has reached out to several playwrights to join the writing staff to help raise the dramatic stakes as well. Meanwhile, Lee Daniels says that Spike Lee has reached out about directing an episode; if he does, he'll join an impressive roster of Hollywood directors that includes John Singleton (*Boyz n the Hood*), Mario Van Peebles (*New Jack City*), and, of course, Daniels himself.

Guest stars will continue to be part of the *Empire* formula, but Strong says they will approach the casting decisions carefully. "I just don't think we need to stunt-cast so much," he told the ATX Fest audience. "As an actor myself, I want to hire people who are talented that were like me and need the job and it's a great opportunity, as opposed to someone who is so famous, that's a fun thing to do for pocket change." The first round of celebrity appearances announced for the new season—including Lenny Kravitz, Chris Rock, and Alicia Keys—seems to confirm the producers are looking for easily recognized stars who won't take too much focus away from the show itself.

The initial hints about plot developments were scant but interesting. Academy Award winner Marisa Tomei will appear in several episodes as billionaire Mimi Whiteman, described by *Deadline* as "a demanding venture capitalist" and "a lover of hip hop music, social trends, high-end fashion and beautiful women." Another addition to the cast, Adam Rodriguez, revealed that he will be playing a paramedic who becomes a new love interest for Cookie. "Cookie and I share a similar affliction that we're battling and we sort of bond over that," he told *E!* "I don't know exactly where that's going to go but I'm hoping it goes to some good places."

Serayah, who plays Tiana on the show, gave *Bustle* a string of emojis as potential spoilers, leading them to speculate that season two will feature "lots and lots of romance," and possibly the return of Naomi Campbell as Camilla. For the most part, however, everyone connected to *Empire* has stuck to one version or another of co-executive producer Wendy Calhoun's remarks at ATX Fest, where she set the stage for "new relationship dynamics," including "relationships that we weren't able to dive into in the first twelve [episodes]."

Before the creative team even got started writing the new episodes, though, show-runner Ilene Chaiken recognized how difficult it would be to keep up with the standard they've set in the first season. "It has to be consistent with the stories we've been telling, and the world that's been created," she said in an interview with Josef Adalian of *Vulture*. "And yet everything has to change, and we have to be better. We absolutely have to be better, and yet we really have to honor what the show is and what's working about it. That is really daunting."

What's also daunting is the huge audience likely to be tuning in for the season premiere, which might even surpass the nearly eighteen million who watched the two-hour finale. It would be the television equivalent of what NPR music critic Chris Molanphy has called "the AC/DC Rule," which explains how "initial sales of an album, particularly a blockbuster, are a referendum on the public's feelings about the act's prior album, not the current one." Case in point: Fans who loved the Australian rock band's *Back in Black* ran out and bought *For Those About to Rock (We Salute You)*, sending it straight to the top of the *Billboard* charts—ultimately, though, it wound up selling fewer copies than its predecessor.

Something similar *could* happen with *Empire*; in fact, many television critics expect that, once viewers see how the cliffhangers from last season are resolved, some of them will move on, and the show's ratings may level out at a slightly lower level. It's a possibility, especially if fans think Daniels and Strong and company have gotten anything wrong and express their displeasure online while the episode is still airing. (March's two-hour season finale, for example, is reported to have generated more than 2.5 million tweets.) If *Empire* goes off the rails, it'll be as big a story as the one that plays out on-screen.

That's a pretty big *if*, though, especially given everything *Empire*'s creative team was able to accomplish in its first season. One thing's for sure: Whatever happens when *Empire* comes back on the air, it's going to be a hell of a lot of fun to watch it all go down.

PHOTO CREDITS

Empire is the breakout hit of 2015, catching everyone—including its own network—off guard as it drew in one of the fastest growing audiences in television history. From the very first episode, viewers have been riveted by the story of record company magnate Lucious Lyon and the struggle within his family for control over Empire Enterprises. Now, as the second season approaches, *Empire: The Unauthorized Untold Story* fills you in on everything you need to know about this powerful drama.

You'll get full backgrounds on Lucious, Cookie, their sons, and all the other major players, including the real-life entertainment icons on whom their stories are based—and learn about the actors who bring the characters to life. You'll get new insights into the Lyon family drama, with detailed analysis of the full first season storyline, and you'll see how Lucious Lyon compares to other great empire builders throughout history. You'll learn about the creative team, led by Timbaland, that created the show's chart-topping musical soundtrack. And you'll get a hint of what the future might hold as *Empire* creators Lee Daniels and Danny Strong prepare to build on their phenomenal opening act.

ROBERT HAM writes about pop culture for a variety of online and print publications, including *Rolling Stone*, *FACT Magazine*, *Stereogum*, *The Oregonian*, *Paste*, and *Alternative Press*. He lives in Portland, Oregon with his wife and son.